The (Practical) Guide to Finding the (Right) Finance Job in Canada

By David Price

Awarded CFA charter, AIMR (2003)
MBA/LLB, Toronto (1999)
BA, McGill (1995)

Library and Archives Canada Cataloguing in Publication

Price, David, 1973-
The practical guide to finding the right finance job in Canada / David Price.

Includes bibliographical references and index.
ISBN 1-896881-55-6
1. Finance—Vocational guidance—Canada. 2. Financial services industry—Vocational guidance—Canada. I. Title.

HG173.P75 2005 332'.023'71 C2005-902081-4

ISBN: 1-896881-55-6

Design: Studio Melrose/Ted Sancton

Printed in Canada

Redlader Publishing is a division of
Price-Patterson Ltd., Canadian Publishers
Montreal, Canada
www.pricepatterson.com

© Copyright 2005. All rights reserved.
  No part of this book may be reproduced in any form without permission from the Publisher.

Important Disclaimer to the Reader

Please realize that the body text is mine. *All the errors and all of the judgments are mine.* The profiled subjects have simply answered the questions posed. They have not approved of my text, nor have they approved of the responses of the other profiled subjects.

Acknowledgements

In Jack Kerouac's *On the Road,* Old Bull Lee divides the world into two groups: "Some's bastards; some's ain't". This book is dedicated to the many *ain'ts* that I've met in the financial profession – some of whom have been gracious enough to help me with this book. I hope all of you make money hand over fist.

For help with the book, many thanks (in chronological order) to Annie Bergevin, Phil Marleau, Tim Price, Richard Bradlow, Cam d., André Charbonneau, John Bradlow, Joe Walewicz, Marc-André Aubé, Scott Fraser, Jean-François Marcoux, Patrick Houston, Patrick Bernes, Ross Gledhill, Rick Hart, Charles Bougie, Louise Lalonde, David Adderley, Andrew Waitman, Martin Kamil, Mila Felcarek, John Bridgman and Pierre Matuszewski.

The world of business generally, and of finance in particular, has received a poor press in recent years. You couldn't blame the unbiased, but unknowledgeable, member of the public for having a bad opinion of finance professionals. Many (or all?) seem wanton, greedy and, above all, selfish. In writing this book, I have only had three refusals to help or be profiled – and one was, I think, out of shyness and another was from a total stranger. Here were busy people with their own careers or businesses to think about who took the time to answer questions and help a friend (or acquaintance, or stranger) out. I can't think of a better refutation of the selfish caricature.

THANK YOU.

Part A: Introduction 9
  1. Purpose 9
  2. Who the hell am I? 10
  3. Terminology Used in this Book 16
  4. Cultures 19
  5. Interview & Career Tips 20

Part B: Recent Events in Canadian Finance 25
  1. The Rise of the Income Trust Market 25
  2. Corporate Governance –
    Operating Companies 30
  3. Compliance – Financial Firms 34

Part C: The Guide 39
  Section I. Career Resources 39
  Section II. The Sell Side 41
    1. Investment Banking 42
      Profiles
        John Bridgman 50
        Jean-François Marcoux 54
      Job Ideas 57
    2. Equity Analysis 59
      Profiles
        Joseph Walewicz 64
        Philippe Marleau 68
      Job Ideas 70
    3. Lending (Corporate Banking) 72
      Profiles
        Pierre Matuszewski 78
        Marc-André Aubé 82
      Job Ideas 86
  A Note on 'Integration' 88
  Section III. The Buy Side 90
    4. Retail Broking 91
      Profiles
        Richard Hart 96
        Timothy E. Price 102
      Job Ideas 106

- 5. Money Management 107
  - Profiles
    - Scott Fraser 114
    - Patrick Bernes 118
  - Job Ideas 120
- Section IV. Private Equity 123
  - 6. Venture Capital 126
    - Profiles
      - Andrew Waitman.................. 130
      - Mila M. Felcarek.................. 132
    - Job Ideas 135
  - 7. Merchant Banking 136
    - Profiles
      - Louise Lalonde.................... 140
      - Charles Bougie.................... 144
    - Job Ideas 147
  - 8. Mezzanine......................... 148
    - Profiles
      - John Bradlow..................... 150
      - Richard Bradlow 154
    - Job Ideas 156
- Section V. Trading 157
  - 9. Trading 157
    - Profiles
      - André Charbonneau................ 162
      - Annie Bergevin.................... 164
      - Patrick Houston................... 166
    - Job Ideas 168

Part D: Some Practical Points 171
1. A Note on the CFA 171
2. A Note on Financial Ratios, Statements
   & Pro Formas 173
3. Microsoft Excel 183

A (Short) Glossary of Terms.................. 186

A (Very Select) Bibliography.................. 189

Index............................... 190

Part A: Introduction

1. Purpose

"There is nothing quite as wonderful as money"
– "The Money Song", Monty Python

"I half relinquished [my previous job in Fidel Castro's government] ... to plunge myself into my apparently God-given gift for finance."
– Che Guevera as quoted in *Che* by Jon Lee Anderson (Grove Press, 1997), p. 447.

I set out to write a book about how to find the *right* finance job in Canada. As our teacher Monty Python reminds us, there may be nothing quite as wonderful as money, but that doesn't necessarily give good career direction to the newly minted BComm or MBA. You may be as enthusiastic as Che Guevera to try your hand at finance (and as confident in your abilities), but that doesn't mean a job will necessarily present itself to you. (Guevera had to overthrow a government to get his finance job!) There are a number of things to keep in mind in the search for that first job.

Firstly, the finance profession is not the only way to make a lot of money. There are other very lucrative professions or businesses. That being said, finance is certainly a good way to make a living and more. The salaries are good, and the bonuses can be better. It is an area where someone with brains and ambition (and maybe just the second) can arrive at the door of a firm with some basic knowledge, no capital, no connections

– and leave wealthy within a fairly short period of time.

Secondly, pursuing a financial career in the wrong way, or in the wrong job, can lead to unhappiness and maybe even unemployment through never getting hired, getting fired or quitting in disgust. The challenge is finding how to put round pegs into round holes. The best way would be to talk to as many people as possible and find out what professions suit you. Your limited time, money and connections may make this approach of marginal value or impossible. To achieve the objective another way, I have assembled some of Canada's most successful finance professionals to talk to you in text about their professions. Every chapter has a more junior and a more senior practitioner – each of whom will have a perspective to add. In addition, there is descriptive material by me and some ideas as to where to send your CV.

2. Who the hell am I?

I was once in your shoes.

I graduated from McGill with a BA in 1995 and went on to graduate from the University of Toronto with MBA and law degrees in 1999. I am from Montreal, Quebec and wanted to return there to work in the finance industry. Given that the 1995 referendum on Quebec independence had almost split the country, people thought that an anglophone returning to Montreal (to work in finance no less!) was just about the stupidest idea that they had ever heard. This viewpoint was shared by my Quebec anglo peers at university and by the guidance staff at U of T. Nevertheless, I did return to Montreal in May 1999 and proceeded to work for five years in the finance industry – before leaving voluntarily in 2004. And four of these years were after the dot.com meltdown. So much for the sceptics.

You don't have to share my specific goals to learn from my experience. My first piece of advice is *do your own homework*. The career guidance people at your university can help, but doing your own digging is an invaluable exercise. You may find opportunities that you didn't even know existed. You may find that a given field is not for you or that going with Firm X over Firm Y is the best choice given your temperament and objectives. Don't assume that Big Bank X in Toronto is the only way to work in finance. There are lots of jobs out there in all sorts of places, fields and firms. Don't curtail your search too early. Like me, you may have specific personal objectives. You may want to work in Vancouver or Calgary or Montreal or Halifax. You may want to work in a small or independent firm. You may – horror of horrors – want to have more free time than a traditional job in your chosen field allows. Don't give up too soon. There are jobs that clearly dominate others (more money for the same sacrifices, same money for smaller sacrifices). There are interesting trade-offs to be made, too: a little less money, a lot less sacrifice; a lot more money, a little more sacrifice. You may believe in efficient markets for stocks, but I would discard any such notion regarding jobs right now.

In the same vein, *treat this book as a starting point only*. I try to explain many different fields for the beginner and not-so-beginner job seeker, but there are a lot of fields and opportunities that I leave out. (Maybe I'll try to be exhaustive in the second edition.)

I always took solace in the fact that I was looking for *just one job*. It sure made the task seem less daunting.

Why am I qualified to write this book?
I've had a lot of experience as a job hunter and finance industry employee, and I've always (out of necessity) done most of my own homework. As an undergrad summer student, I worked one summer as an (agency basis) equity trader and one summer as an (agency basis) bond trader for the retail brokerage firm of MacDougall, MacDougall & MacTier. (It is one of Canada's oldest independent firms and has branches in Montreal, Toronto, Quebec City and London, Ontario.) While I never managed my own position, I have some understanding of how a trading desk works and how it feels to work in that (hectic) atmosphere.

As a business and law student, I worked as an equity analyst for Dlouhy Investments (now Versant Partners). For one summer, my 'sector' (if you can call it that) was ultra-junior, speculative stocks. (Only one of the four stocks is still trading.) Once again, covering penny stocks for a summer is not the same as covering companies with billion dollar market caps for years, but at least I have some idea of what the job entails. (I was also working side-by-side with other equity analysts.)

After graduation from business and law at U of T, I worked for the investment banking operation of one of Canada's chartered banks. I worked mainly in mergers and acquisitions (M&A). In addition to learning the basic operations of that kind of shop, I was able to witness at first hand the final (1999-2000) folly of the dot.com bubble. (The internet was so new, by the way, that even as the dot.com frenzy reached its peak in March 2000, there were fairly young guys – late 20's – working with me who, when they started working, had *sent away by mail* for annual reports just to be able to do basic research on a given company.) In the same era, one Canadian company almost turned up its nose at an IPO valuation based on 15 times *revenue* because it was grossly inferior to then-current American valuation multiples. Another company had a market cap of approximately $1.5 billion with no track record of revenue (never mind profits) and multiples that, when calculated on *projected* revenue, were in the double digits. Another amusing aside regarding the world of the dot.com's was the emergence of the 'LQA' (last quarter annualized) metric as a way to measure revenue, EBITDA, profit etc … The idea was that the most recently completed year of a company's operating results was not a good measurement of its financial health or size due to the rapid growth it was experiencing. The solution? Take the last quarter of results and multiply by four! I have not heard, but I don't think this measurement has survived to today. My time in investment banking definitely gave me some perspective on that industry (including its non-dot.com, unsilly aspects), as did my next job.

After being fired from investment banking due to a clash with the eventual Montreal branch manager, I obtained a job at a mid-market merchant bank. (Merchant banks buy and sell private companies for profit, somewhat like what mutual funds do with the shares of public companies.) The firm was in the final stages of closing a new, larger fund and specialized in what were still called 'old economy' companies when I arrived there in late 2000. As time went on, the 'sexiness' of the old economy increased dramatically. That job went better than my previous post and I stayed for 3½ years. Unfortunately, they decided to meet some internal challenges by taking on more staff – an idea that I thought was bad in principle and would affect me detrimentally on a day-to-day basis. When I was told of the change, I knew it was time to go. So I left two days later.

Nevertheless, the merchant banking job gave me a lot of insight into a lot of finance fields. Obviously, I was witnessing (and doing) merchant banking at first hand. I was also an observer of investment banking (now at the mid-market level, but the methods and stratagems don't change that much) because investment bankers were pitching us deals on a daily basis (on the new investment side) and we would employ them to sell our existing portfolio companies (on the exit side). I was also taking a fairly close look at corporate banking and the world of mezzanine debt because virtually every merchant banking deal involves borrowing senior debt (to effect the purchase of the prospective portfolio company) and setting up an operating line (for the newly re-launched company to draw upon for its seasonal – or other – swings). A merchant banking deal may also involve borrowing mezzanine debt to help finance the acquisition.

You will detect a whiff (or more than that) of cynicism in this book. I would not recommend that you be as flippant in your interviews or work life as I am in the text, but I don't see how a thinking person can stay sane without finding and sharing the humour in some of the nonsense that goes on in the world of finance. And there is a lot of nonsense that has gone on. I am also sure it will continue. Some of it is well documented – Enron, Nortel, dot.com's etc ... – and some isn't, trust me.

Nevertheless, depending on your objectives and temperament, it may be the right industry for you – and I'm sure other industries are not without material problems of their own. There is a lot of money, prestige and fun to be had in finance (which do you seek?) and among the nitwits, nincompoops and not-so-nice people, there are good and intelligent individuals to work for and with. Make what you will of it – and use the book as a guide.

Just to complete my saga, after leaving the merchant bank, my father and I decided to re-launch his publishing company, Price-Patterson Ltd., and we went on the hunt for new projects. I knew a lot about the finance industry and knew there was a void in the supply of guides from my time as a job-hunter. Hence the book. I hope it proves useful to you.

David Price
Montreal, June 2005

3. Terminology Used in this Book

'Company'

In this book, I have used the word 'company' to mean 'operating company' (i.e. a company that manufactures, distributes or retails physical objects; or offers non-financial services; and that will have occasion to use the services of a financial firm from time to time). A person who works in 'industry' (i.e. for a company) is usually referred to as an 'operator'. I will adhere to this usage in my book.

'Firm'

I have used the term 'firm' to mean a financial entity of some kind. The firm may be a chartered bank with a full service offering, an investment dealer with a seat on the exchange that offers many ancillary services, a money management partnership whose assets consist of desks, phones and management agreements with its money-possessing clients or a boutique investment bank of one or two professionals with no repeat clients whatsoever and no assets to speak of. Regardless of what form they take, it is these firms that are your prospective employers.

'Private equity'

I have used 'private equity' to describe one of my sections in The Guide. In my usage, it includes three activities (venture capital, merchant banking and mezzanine lending). In fact, you will find that 'private equity' is more often used in the world of finance as a synonym for 'merchant banking' or 'buyouts'. I will stick to my own usage, however, because I find it convenient to have a single term to describe three activities that have so much in common from a *structural* point of view (e.g. they raise money in time limited-funds, they invest that money in a finite number of deals and return most of it to their investors; they earn management fees and 'carry' at the expense of those investors etc ...). See Section IV, Private Equity, below. Even *substantively*, they are quite similar: each activity is focussed on investing in the equity/quasi-equity of private companies and on a medium-term exit. This similarity has been acknowledged by the market itself: some firms have more than one private equity activity under one roof, e.g. venture capital, merchant banking, mezzanine lending (Edgestone); venture capital and merchant banking (NovaCap). An investment opportunity that comes in the door might not work for the initially targeted fund, but may work for its sister fund down the hall. Fundraising, reporting to a common pool of investors and back office activities can also be professionalized and shared by the various funds. To make things even more confusing, in England 'merchant bank' used to refer to firms that underwrote securities (i.e. investment banking or corporate finance), but did not trade them or have a seat on the exchange (See Paul Ferris – *Gentlemen of Fortune*, p. 172-3).

'Strategic' and 'Financial'

In the M&A field, there is a usually a distinction made between a 'strategic' and 'financial' investor. A strategic investor is a company that is already active in the industry in which the investee or target company operates. When Rogers bought Microcell, it was acting as a strategic investor. A financial investor, on the other hand, has money (and maybe lots of other things, too, like financial structuring expertise and relevant operating experience among its staff), but no operating assets in the relevant industry and no long-term mandate to be in a particular industry. When the Ontario Teachers' Pension Plan Board (usually just known as 'Teachers') and KKR bought the Yellow Pages from Bell, they were acting as financial investors.

'Due Diligence'

'Due diligence' began life as a term to describe the investigation of a company that underwriters of securities must complete in order to fulfil their statutory responsibilities (see p. 45, below). It is now used by just about any investor to describe a spectrum of investigative activities. In the original, underwriting/corporate finance context, due diligence is thorough, but perfunctory. The investment bankers bringing an issue to market do not intend to own it for years to come: they just want the prospectus they sign to be true. In the case of a new bond from a repeat issuer, due diligence can mean a few questions over the phone by a junior banker. In the strategic acquirer, merchant banking or venture capital context, due diligence can mean the investing group's initial look-see at a file, or the full-on investigation done with the help of third party lawyers, accountants and industry experts. In the context of senior and mezzanine lending, due diligence is a blend of the lender's own work and piggy-backing on work done by the equity sponsors (VC, merchant bank or strategic) and the sponsors' professionals (lawyers, accountants, industry experts).

4. Cultures

As a former participant, a large part of the insider's view that I want to share are my impressions of the different cultures that exist inside the different fields that I cover in this book. In *Liar's Poker*, Michael Lewis indirectly advises his reader to "love your corporate culture." I would go a bit further: you can learn to love a given culture, or learn to deal with it, or learn to avoid it. Knowing about given cultures should be useful in a number of ways. Firstly, use the information for your interviews. Present yourself correctly for the given field. Also, know what to expect from interviewers from that field. Secondly, use my views (and those of others) to help decide what you want to do. If you're shy and retiring, avoid the fields where the outgoing and garrulous abound. In addition, find out more information. Ask non-interviewers whom you meet (I don't recommend you chat so frankly with interviewers) if I'm right and add to your knowledge base.

If you sat down with one representative person from each of the nine fields in this guide who happened to make the same amount of money, be the same age and have the same status in their field, *they would still be very different from one another*. They might all be self-confident, in the bad cases arrogant, but in different ways. Every culture is unique and evaluates its practitioners according to its own code. As Nietzche might say, "A table of values hangs over every people." A less high brow example: in the movie *My American Cousin*, some of the local Canadian boys evaluate the 'American cousin' of the title after a day of work in the fruit orchards of the Okanagan. One of them says, "He's okay, but not much of a cherry picker." What is an expression of contempt in the rest of the world is a sign of manhood to them. (And the good old boys are right: picking cherries isn't easy.) Every main field here also has its own standard. Govern yourself accordingly.

You'll find my views on culture at the end of each chapter, except for the three private equity fields which I deal with in the section introduction.

5. Interview & Career Tips

Here is some more generic advice:

Apply early and often. Even if the prospects of getting a summer job are not great, go through the exercise with as many firms as possible. The more you do interviews, the better you will be and the more you will be able to improve. The same goes for full time jobs. If you have done a few interviews before the ones you really care about, you may be that much sharper come game day.

Read the newspaper and have a little story to talk about if asked. I was asked this once and didn't have a sufficiently 'financial' story for the interviewer's taste. On the other hand, I was also once told by an interviewer that he was unimpressed by people who asked him for his views on bank mergers and the Asian meltdown (hot topics in 1999). You gotta judge it.

Ask for cards or names. I was once asked by a second interviewer who my first interviewer had been. I hadn't caught the name and looked foolish. Did it matter who the first guy was? Not one bit, but it looked bad. Ask for the names of people you meet. Repeat them. Ask for their business cards so you know for sure.

Do your homework. Although it is a totally phoney exercise and irrelevant to the work you are being hired to do, find out 'stuff' about the firm you are applying to. When you first begin working, your work will be fairly generic from a skills point of view ('here's an MBA, here's the work an MBA can do') and specific ('work on this particular transaction'), but, for some reason, knowing about the firm's largest clients or recent deals or special expertise or executives is considered important in interviews. I was hired by a chartered bank and did not know the name of the CEO. It didn't matter at all (who cares who the grand poobah is?), but I'm glad my ignorance didn't come to light in an interview.

Get an inside track. Try to find out about your target firm's recent deals, reputation etc ... If it comes up, you'll have something to say.

Have a card. I find it really cheesy, but having a 'business' card even while you're a student is a good gimmick. If you meet someone on the fly, you can give them your coordinates instantly and reliably. One of these nibbles might be the right job for you. (And, as a friend pointed out, you can always use your card to pass your phone number to a potential romantic liaison.)

Follow up with a call. In the case of the large bank-owned firms, calling up your interviewers a few days after the interview is probably a waste of time and may even annoy them. In the case of smaller firms, following up may make the difference between getting hired or not, and may even make the difference between them offering *anyone* a job or not. Decision-makers at small shops have a lot on their minds. Don't let them forget about you.

Don't rely on HR. I have found that dealing exclusively with the human resources people is a bad strategy. They will not make final decisions about candidates. They will not have to work shoulder-to-shoulder with you. Use them as a resource. They often coordinate the efforts of the larger firms. Make sure, however, that you get into contact with a professional in the department you want to work in.

If you're trying to find a job at a branch office, make sure you have contact with both HQ and the branch. You need to be known to head office because many branch offices aren't allowed to go to the bathroom without head office permission. You need to be known to the branch because if they don't know about you, they won't be able to ask to go to the bathroom. Even so, be prepared to field questions about spending time (3-12 months) at head office before being allowed to work in the branch of your choice.

A final hopeful note.
Remember these guys put their pants on one leg at a time. During my i-banker training session at a large chartered bank, we had to do presentations regarding a case. We were supposed to get mucky-mucks from high up in the bank to watch the final presentations, but they couldn't make it, so we got people from the 'class' immediately ahead of us. There was a very impressive looking, Superman look-alike who took delight in grilling the incoming trainees. I didn't see the point in kowtowing to a guy one year ahead on the corporate ladder so when he barked, I barked back. My instincts were right. He was fired about a year before they got around to firing me. You should be prudent and polite with all the interviewers you meet, but, remember, they could be roadkill in a year or two.

Also, don't be intimidated by the supposed sophistication of the firms you are trying to join. During my time at a *major Canadian financial institution*, I was asked to compile a list of deals we had done with a particular client (also, as it happens, a major Canadian company). When my survey of the files and of the staff was finished, there were still many missing deals. To complete my task, I was told to go around the office and examine the 'tombstones' that are printed in the newspaper when a deal is done and that underwriters frame and put on their walls. These were the only records left! I wish our prospective client could have seen his 'information age' financial advisers at work.

In a similar vein, in *Gentlemen of Fortune* (p. 240), Ferris tells a story where a third party banker gets paid a fee for introducing two divisions of the *same bank* to each other.

Don't be intimidated by the interview process. It is run by the same people.

My one career tip

Apart from what I have said already about knowing as much as possible before you begin, I would think seriously about going to a large firm at the start of your career – regardless of where you want to end up. I worked at a small branch office of a major firm that happened to disintegrate when I was there. As a result, I know people at firms all over the street. Others can get the same kind of exposure by going to a larger office from which people leave at a more normal pace. Regardless, such a network is great for information, deal flow, job intelligence and so on. I would recommend you giving some serious thought about this future networking before you sign your first job offer.

Part B:
Recent Events in Canadian Finance

1. The Rise of the Income Trust Market

A major event in the last five years has been the rise and rise of the income trust market. It has gone from a market capitalization of approximately $10 billion in 1996[1], to approximately $45 billion in 2002, to one of approximately $130 billion in March 2005.[2] New issues of income trust units grew from 33 deals totalling $1.5 billion in 1999 to 170 deals totalling $17 billion in 2004.[3] What is going on here?

An income trust is an 'anti-dot.com'. Dot.com's offered almost nothing today (sometimes no revenue, almost always no profits) and promised the world tomorrow (spectacular growth, eventual profitability, sale to a strategic buyer at a huge premium – the works). For good reasons, people got sick of that. They then went running for the opposite: not much growth, no prospect of a sale to a strategic – but profits. Profits yesterday, profits today, profits tomorrow. And not just profits, but free cash flow to be enjoyed now; free cash to be distributed quarterly or even monthly; free cash flow everywhere. This market continues to grow and mature, although there are a few clouds on the horizon. As you will see below, much of

---

[1] Source: Canadian Association of Income Funds/RBC Capital Markets "Presentation on Foreign Ownership Restrictions" (September 2004).
[2] Source: Genuity/York University LLB/MBA Conference "The Future of Income Trusts in Canada" – Draft (March 8, 2005).
[3] Source: IDA "Review of Equity New Issues and Trading" (Feb. 7, 2005).

the impetus behind income trusts is tax savings-based. The governments that lose out on those taxes may eventually look askance at the whole phenomenon. In addition, placing large amounts of the Canadian economy into a no-growth/low-growth mode may prove to be a problem. (Income trusts are allowed to grow, but must pay out a large portion of their profits, so organic growth will almost always be modest. Even growth by acquisition must be done in a way that preserves the flow of cash to the unitholders, because those unitholders are there for cash, not the promise of future cash.) Investors may eventually tire of low growth and undo the trust structures, or government may decide that it knows better than the investing public and put up regulatory obstacles to curb the growth of the market. Lastly, there are unresolved issues surrounding the limited liability of investors in income trusts, although these seem to be minor – and Ontario recently resolved them in favour of investors.

What is an income trust?

An income trust is a publicly traded business whose chief aim is to return income to its 'unitholders' on a consistent and long-term (or even perpetual) basis.

A trust is a different kind of legal entity from a corporation. The original idea behind a trust was that one party (the trustee) had legal ownership (i.e. control) of an asset or assets, and a second party (the beneficiary) had the right to the *benefits* of that asset (i.e. the profits or income or use of it). A trust was often designed (or forced by law) to liquidate at some future date. Once the original beneficiary (or beneficiaries) died or reached the age of majority or re-married, the assets would then pass – unfettered this time – to the 'residual' beneficiary. Eventually, there were all kinds of applications for trusts in personal estate planning (e.g. to protect – or protect against – spendthrift children or greedy surviving spouses), for charitable organizations, for tax planning etc ...

Corporations, on the other hand, were originally designed to limit the liability of individual investors to the amount actually invested in a given business. The idea was to induce investors to risk *some* money by making it clear they were not unintentionally risking *all* their money. Unlike trusts, corporations soon 'housed' many huge businesses that were making lots of money. Surprise, surprise, this corporate wealth soon attracted governments' interest and they eventually set up income taxes at the corporate level. There are all kinds of ways to tax corporations, but, basically, corporations were taxed on profits whether they distributed those profits to their shareholders or not. Often those distributed profits (i.e. dividends) would be taxed again in the hands of the investors. For this reason, there was very little incentive to distribute profits to shareholders and so dividends became less and less of a feature of public corporation life. (The desire to grow the business at even tiny rates of growth – in order to build a bigger business for management to run – may also have been a reason for holding profits inside a corporation.)

Eventually, people started to notice that some businesses made so much money and had such little use for it that it was crazy to hold it in a corporation and pay tax on it – especially when some of the shareholders were either completely tax exempt (e.g. pension funds) or exempt due to the type of account they used to hold the investment (e.g. an RRSP). What a shame, people thought, that those profits without any use inside the business couldn't go directly to the tax exempt shareholders!

What were these strange businesses that made so much money and had no use for it? The answer, at first, was oil wells. Once an oil well had been discovered and was operational, it became a completely different kind of business from the exploration company it had been at inception. Sure, all the profits could go into more exploration, but that was kind of like endlessly doubling down at the blackjack table. It made more sense to run the oil well as a mature business and let those investors who wanted the risk to invest in other exploration companies.

What was the answer? A non-corporate entity that would not have to pay tax on profits if it distributed them to its investors. There were two candidates: the partnership and the trust. In both cases, the tax code allowed distributed profits to be taxed only in the hands of the ultimate investor. For reasons that I won't get into, the trust won as the vehicle of choice and all of those profits of properly transformed corporations were now taxed only in the hands of the investors. Some sort of entity (often a management company) performed the role of 'trustee' and the investors became the 'beneficiaries'. Evidence of their 'beneficiary' status was demonstrated by a 'unit' in the trust, so they became 'unitholders'.

(Unlike corporations and that partnership/corporation hybrid, the limited partnership, trusts did not have built-in limited liability. For this reason, it was often necessary to insert a corporation into the structure to own the actual business asset and so limit the liability of the various parties (i.e. trustee and beneficiaries). The income of the corporation could then be 'stripped' on a tax deductible basis from the corporation via a large debt instrument held by the trust in the corporation and *then* distributed to the investors.)

As investors recovered from the dot.com hangover (see above), they began to wonder if income trusts couldn't be applied to other kinds of businesses. The answer has been an almost unequivocal "yes". Hamburger chains, pulp and paper mills, generic household products and all sorts of other businesses have all been turned into income trusts.

The future of this instrument is, of course, unwritten.

2. Corporate Governance – Operating Companies

'Corporate governance' is a topic that has received a lot of press in the last few years. Basically, the goal of good corporate governance is to make sure that the company in question behaves well: i.e. obeys laws that carry punishments, does not open itself up to lawsuits, maintains a good public profile and, within these constraints, makes as much money as possible for (all of) its shareholders. This may seems simple. It is not. Let's consider two aspects.

(Most of the following discussion applies best to public companies, although there can be governance issues inside private companies – especially if there is more than one shareholder or if the shareholder base and management team are distinct.)

The board of directors. The buck stops at the board. It is the board that hires and fires managers, sets broad policies, okays budgets and must agree to important decisions (e.g. acquisitions, mergers/sales, stock issues, new debt). In an ideal world, the board would be an objective and interested third party with all the time and resources needed to do its job, but the board consists of people who confront possible obstacles to attaining this ideal.

Firstly, it is a long tradition in Canada (and elsewhere) that management has seats on the board. Indeed, the highest post for a paid, full time manager in many companies is not CEO or president, but 'chairman' – i.e. chairman of the board. This is not a crazy situation. Often, managers own a large part of their company. Why shouldn't they be represented? Even if not, managers may have a lot to contribute at board meetings. They, after all, know the company best – seeing as they run it 24/7. Unfortunately, having managers on the board compromises its perfect objectivity. In practice, this theoretical conflict may not be an issue, but it can lead to all sorts of problems. The board member/managers may vote for inappropriate compensation (including expense accounts, options or bonus thresholds). They may expand the company so as to increase its size, regardless of the return on equity. And they will never vote to fire themselves.

As a second group and brake on these possibilities, let's consider the independent directors. Increasingly, it is becoming necessary to have them on boards and to have them be, or be exclusively, on key board committees (e.g. audit, compensation). The problem with independent directors is that board duties have traditionally been supplementary to full time jobs or adjuncts to a retired businessperson's life. An independent board member is not 'on the job' full time, nor do they have vast resources, nor do they work on site at the company in question. As a result, their level of oversight is inevitably constrained. In addition, they are not management. They may never have worked at the company in question or even in the relevant industry. As a result, the level of detailed knowledge they bring to the job is also constrained.

Accounting scandals. This issue is really a subset of corporate governance. Good corporate governance will include good audit policies and procedures so that accounting is done properly. But why is accounting so rife with problems – e.g. the case of a major Canadian tech company clawing back US$8.6 million in bonuses awarded on the basis of faulty accounting?

Firstly, accounting is not a strict code of rules. Management sets accounting policies that must be blessed as being within GAAP (generally accepted accounting principles), but that doesn't mean that one rule applies. As a result, managers and companies will generally choose those policies that are best for them. Problems, of course, arise when choosing between different accounting presentations goes too far and becomes fraudulent. And the temptation comes from objective gains to be realized. Depending on when and how revenue, costs and capital expenditures are presented, there may be tax savings, debt rating advantages, stock market pricing gains, bonus gains (to managers) and profit shifting (forward and backward to make the present or the future look better than it really is or will be) – and all this is before outright fraud and theft.

A number of measures have been proposed and implemented including having more independent directors (by securities law fiat or stock exchange rules). In the US, the Sarbanes-Oxley Act, passed in the wake of the Enron and WorldCom debacles, contains a number of provisions, but those requiring CEO and CFO certificates approving financial statements and protecting/empowering/forcing disclosure on auditors, audit committees, corporate counsel and whistle-blowers are most relevant to the present discussion.

I believe that all these problems result from a fundamental tension. On the one hand, the public markets crave the growth that management-owned, management-led, management-incentivized companies can deliver. No one wants to invest with bureaucrats who draw a salary and have no interest in the performance of their stock. On the other hand, the public market demands a certain transparency. 'Widows and orphans' can and do invest in these companies. Even sophisticated money managers need to be able to take financial statements at face value and believe in the basic honesty of management. The cost of individual due diligence is simply too high, and reducing that cost is much of the reason for public markets in the first place. It seems to me that a simple solution would be to require that no officer of a public company be a board member and that all board members be compensated entirely with stock (escrowed until they are no longer board members) bought at market prices over their tenure. There doesn't seem to be the will to make this kind of change (and there would be strong opposition from Canada's many family-controlled companies), but the pendulum has definitely swung in the direction of stricter rules, greater transparency and more accountability. One friend of mine has commented that it is sometimes hard to find real news stories (i.e. about company performance) in the newspaper because of all the 'corporate governance' stories.

As a job applicant, be aware of these issues and of the new regulatory context.

3. Compliance – Financial Firms

Financial firms have also had a slew of regulatory/legal problems and bad publicity. To consider a few:
- In the world of retail broking, a major bank has recently been in the news because one of its brokers created a situation where the trades of one account were guaranteed by another client – allegedly without the 'guarantor' client's informed or actual permission.
- There have been many cases of inappropriate investing by retail brokers.
- In 2004, four Canadian mutual funds and three Canadian brokerage houses were fined for insufficient vigilance regarding/complicity in 'market timing'.[4] In 2003, Eliot Spitzer, the Attorney Gen-

---

[4] 'Market timing' in this specific sense is possible because mutual funds set their entry/redemption price once a day at the end of trading. The practice involves one of two things. In the first case, sometimes called 'late trading', there is outright fraud: individuals backdate trades in order to buy mutual fund units at a low closing price knowing that good news has come out since closing. The damage to the other unitholders is from sharing this gain with unitholders who have invested in the fund by fraudulent means, i.e. dilution. The other kind of marketing timing (and the one at issue in the Canadian case) is more subtle. Individuals buy units of a mutual fund at an entry price that is 'stale', i.e. likely low given currently known data. Funds that trade non-North American securities (e.g. Asian) can have stale closing prices because the stocks they hold cease trading before the mutual fund's unit price for that day will be determined and trade afterwards (during North America's night). If North American markets have done well, it is likely that Asian markets will, too, so (indirectly) buying Asian securities at today's closing price makes sense. The goal is to sell the unit the next day for a quick profit. The damage done to long-term unitholders is in the increased transaction costs to the mutual fund of these many,

eral of New York State, accused at least nine American firms of the practice, including more serious forms of it, i.e. late trading.
- In 2000, the pension management arm of one of the chartered banks was found to be surreptitiously buying stock in companies in which it already held shares at quarter ends in order to drive up the price and so be able to report slightly better performance for the assets it was managing.
- In the United States especially, the following have also been hot topics, many of them the subject of cases emanating from New York State Attorney General Eliot Spitzer's office and/or (often subsequently) the SEC:
  - the way hot, 'likely to pop' (i.e. pop upwards) IPOs were allocated between clients, also called 'spinning' – problem: some investing clients being favoured over others, corporate clients not receiving the best pricing they could have from their issue;
  - retail brokers recommending mutual funds that paid them do so;
  - analysts being insufficiently independent from their firms' investment banking departments and being effectively forbidden from being negative about underwriting clients and/or being

---

large volume trades that is not shared by the market timers – and from the dilution as described above (although in this case, the gain is shared with people who are not acting fraudulently). A fund's strategy and required cash reserves will also be distorted by market timers. Interestingly, market timing is not illegal for the practitioners, but funds are required to protect their clients from it. It was a simple failure to do so (by not enforcing published fee penalties for frequent trading) that earned the Canadian funds censure from the OSC.

required to be positive – problem: conflict of interest, biased research;
- analysts being outright dishonest (e.g. privately disparaging companies they publicly recommended) or incompetent (not doing sufficient research into an investment idea).

Some of these abuses are indefensible (incompetence: e.g. buying inappropriate investments, inadequate research; breaches of trust: e.g. doing things beyond the scope of one's mandate; dishonesty: e.g. publicly recommending things that privately one doesn't, backdating trades), but, like in the world of operating companies/public issuers, in many cases the conflict is built into the system. The large chartered banks in Canada and the large banks in the United States have gone into all areas of finance (i.e. representing/ servicing individuals, securities-issuing companies and other market participants – as well as speculating/ investing themselves). In many respects, clients and stockholders of these firms should benefit. It is convenient for the consumer to have a chequing account, brokerage account and mutual fund family under one roof. Investors are keen to participate in hot IPOs and being the client of a retail broker whose firm also has an underwriting arm increases one's chances of being able to invest. From the point of view of the firms' shareholders, there are massive synergies to be realized. The more services are offered under one roof, the better overhead can be shared and the more likely that a given client's need is going to be satisfied in-house. The problem, of course, is that as firms try to maximize synergies, lines can become crossed. Equity analysts becoming, in effect, investment bankers is one such manifestation. Rewarding preferred clients with share allocations of a hot IPO is another.

On another front, there is so much behaviour that seems innocuous at the time or in small quantities, that isn't so when it becomes widespread. Buying shares of an issuer in which you already own stock may not seem dastardly, but if the intention is to manipulate the stock price, then it is. Having third party clients come in and out of your mutual fund does not seem like wrongdoing, but if other clients suffer because of it and if you do not enforce rules you put in place to protect them, you are in the wrong. As Eliot Spitzer says, "The cases against Wall Street are like stopping someone speeding on a highway: the other cars slow down for a while, and then, after a certain number of miles, they speed up again. The question is, 'How many miles before they start speeding again?'"

As with the case of corporate governance and my proposal for a strict division of management from board, a simple solution would seem to be prohibiting firms from representing both companies (via investment banking) and individuals (via retail brokers, money managers or mutual funds). While this wouldn't get rid of the cases of outright fraud or negligence or incompetence, it would get rid of most conflicts of interest. Once again, there is not the will to create this kind of solution. Nevertheless, the trend is definitely towards more regulation and more scrutiny. Two friends of mine have commented that 'compliance' is decreasing the enjoyment they used to take in their work.

As a job applicant, be aware of the major conflicts of interest, of the remedies that have been put in place to curtail their influence and of the new importance placed on being squeaky clean.

Part C: The Guide

Section I. Career Resources

There are three main ways to apply to a firm:
#1 On campus recruiting
#2 Talking to human resources ('HR') at head office (usually Toronto)
#3 Talking directly to the professionals you will be working for

As the individualism of your job search increases (or as the firm you want to work for decreases in size or number of hirees per year), the more important #3 will be. If you want to work in investment banking in Toronto at a major bank (and have the grades and background to do so), #1 will do just fine. If you want to work in a specific group or office or for a smaller firm, it is going to be #3 all the way. Remember that even in the case of a large firm with a very involved HR-driven hiring process, the professionals will make the final decisions. That is the contact that matters.

My original idea for this book was to have a list of firms, contact names and addresses at the end of each chapter toward which to direct CVs. I called one or two of the major banks to start creating the list and was told that, before they divulged this precious information, it would have to be cleared through 'Communications' or, in one case, 'Legal'. Given constantly changing personnel at the target firms and each job candidate's specific goals (e.g. one specific department among many, specific city preferences etc …) this information would have been marginally useful at best, so instead I have put together a list of employment ideas and possible resources. If there is an easy route to apply for a firm (e.g. the large banks always hire a large-ish number of investment bankers, corporate bankers and equity analysts from business school), it will be easy to find the most up to date information on campus or on their website. For the other, more individualistic cases, you will be looking for a very specific piece of information, e.g. who at Small Firm A hires for the investment banking department of the Calgary office? It will most often be the actual professional you want to work for – make sure to talk to him.

Section II. The Sell Side

The sell side is so called because participants are focussed on selling financial instruments to managers of money (be they retail brokers, money managers, pension funds or mutual funds). All aspects of finance are competitive, but the sell side is particularly so, because none of its business repeats without winning a mandate afresh. An investment banking advisor may be hired for one transaction and never hired again. Even companies with established investment banking relationships shop around or invite newcomers to compete for business in order to keep the incumbent honest. They also divide business between firms. In terms of equity trade execution (one of the wealth generators for equity analysts), an equity buyer can turn on a dime or split business with perfect ease. All the competing dealers are a phone call away. Even lenders can be (and are) replaced through refinancings or at the time of a major corporate event. (On the buy side, relationships between the manager of money and the money-possessing client can last undisturbed for decades.)

1. Investment Banking

Investment banking is the business of providing advice to companies regarding the procurement and deployment of capital. It can be divided into three categories:
- Corporate finance
- Mergers & Acquisitions (M&A)
- Specialized disciplines

Corporate finance

Investment bankers who work in the corporate finance sector help companies raise money (in the past often called 'underwriting' their securities). Generally, the investment banking firm is paid a percentage of the money raised. As the money-raising mandate in question increases in complexity or difficulty (especially due to the company's riskiness or lack of track record), the percentage paid to the investment bank increases. Debt usually carries a lesser fee percentage than equity. The money raised can be for new projects (capital expenditures or the acquisition of whole companies) or capital restructuring: e.g. paying off old debt with new debt, paying off debt with equity, raising debt to buy back equity.

M&A

Investment bankers who work in M&A advise companies how, when and whether to buy whole companies or sell their company (or parts of it) to new shareholders. Generally, the investment banking firm is paid a percentage of the final transaction's value. A transaction's 'value' can be the equity value or the enterprise value (the sum of the company's equity and debt). The allocation of progressively smaller percentages of this amount is often called a 'Lehman formula'. The original Lehman formula may have been fixed in terms of equity value or enterprise value, thresholds and actual percentages, but I have seen many permutations used.

Specialized disciplines

One area that has grown immensely in the last few years has been 'structured finance'. This includes two similar fields: securitization and structured finance proper. Securitization is the bundling and sale/quasi-sale of a company's accounts receivable to third party investors. The idea is that the company gets a lower cost of funds by selling the receivables today (and, say, paying down its debt with the proceeds) than it would by holding the receivables until collection date (and keeping its debt at a higher level). There can also be collateral benefits (e.g. a 'smaller' balance sheet attracts less capital tax, less debt on the balance sheet can present a better picture of the firm from the point of view of GAAP accounting). Structured finance involves a similar idea (i.e. selling operating assets), but applied to fixed assets. An example would be a company selling one of its factories to third party investors and then immediately leasing it back. The implied cost of the lease should end up being lower than owning the asset and financing it oneself with, say, debt. Investment bankers in this field advise companies how to execute these (often complex) transactions so that all the transaction's goals are in fact met.

The day-to-day work of an investment banker involves a lot 'pitching' – i.e. looking for new mandates. The investment bankers begin by coming up with an idea. They may think it is a good time for a company to raise money or make an acquisition. They may know that a given company's debt is nearing maturity and needs to be refinanced. They may know that a new management team is more aggressive on the M&A front than their predecessors. A lot of time is spent making a 'pitch book' that will explain the idea to the prospective client. The pitch book will explain the idea by showing what the investment banker thinks is going on in the market and how the company in question should react. Comparable company analysis (or 'comps') is a quick and ubiquitous method. For instance, if a company (and/or its sector) is enjoying a high multiple (the most frequently used multiple is enterprise value / EBITDA – for a discussion of EBITDA see p. 177, below), the banker may advocate issuing equity. If an industry is consolidating, the banker may recommend buying rival firms or selling out to a strong consolidator. If a company is suffering from a low multiple in comparison to its peers, the investment banker might come with ideas to correct the situation. There are many possible solutions. Sometimes a company's float (i.e. the dollar value of freely tradeable shares) is too small for large institutions to buy and trade shares. The solution might be to issue new shares or do a secondary (i.e. the sale of shares by a large existing shareholder – often an owner-founder). A company may be in too many businesses for the market's taste or understanding. The solution might be to break up the company through asset sales or through partial equity offerings of the component companies or through spin-offs. Investment bankers sometimes suck and blow at the same time. One company may be urged to sell shares in some of its subsidiaries in order to get 'full value' for them while, the next day, another company may be told that the parent company is being hit with a 'holding company discount' for owning independently traded companies. Whatever works.

The hit ratio of pitches to signed mandates is low, but once a mandate is signed, the bankers go to work – for pay this time. In the case of a corporate finance mandate, they organize the company's information for prospective investors and present it. For public issues of stock and debt, a formal, legally defined document called a prospectus must often be written. The prospectus describes the business and outlines the risk to the unsophisticated retail investor. Prospectus-writing is shared by the investment bankers and the lawyers. For an initial public offering of stock (an 'IPO'), the marketing material can include a full, public-oriented 'roadshow'. Buy-siders and their clients receive all sorts of glossy material about the company and why investors should buy its shares. Very importantly in the case of public issues of stock or debt, investment bankers do their 'due diligence' (asking questions, touring facilities etc …) before signing the prospectus. Securities law imposes some responsibility for the truth of the prospectus on the investment bank. By having done due diligence before signing it, they fulfil this statutory obligation and have a defence if sued. For a private placement (as opposed to a publicly-retailed issue), the company may approach only a few institutional investors.

In the case of an M&A mandate, a lot of time is spent on valuation. The investment bankers do a lot of work trying to give their client the value of the target and/or the value of their own company. The first cut is with public information. As the transaction progresses more and better information comes to light, requiring revision of the model or models. Frequently, they create a full, discounted cash flow model ('DCF') of the company and/or of the merged company. When the company in question needs to raise money to complete an acquisition, the M&A mandate can include a corporate finance aspect. The firm has be a wary buyer *and* be ready to sell itself and the merged company to prospective investors. Investment bankers do the underlying financial analysis, present it to their client and potential investors, help coordinate all the other professionals who get involved as the transaction takes shape (e.g. lawyers, accountants) and supervise the closing.

In poor markets, the ratio of signed mandates to closed deals deteriorates. In the corporate finance field, deals can fail when investors do not want to buy shares at all or demand overly low pricing in the eyes of company management. In the M&A field, the deal can fall apart for all sorts of reasons: disagreement on pricing, poor chemistry between the buying management and the target management, inability to raise the funds needed to close the acquisition, the non-monetary terms of the sale, legal issues (anti-trust, securities law).

Culture

"There's always been in this market a crazy relationship between prestige and profit, the two Ps. At times demand for visibility and market share runs ahead of a concern over profitability."

– anonymous investment banker quoted in Paul Ferris' *Gentlemen of Fortune* (p. 113)

Investment bankers spend *a lot* of time together. Investment banking hours are long and often include dinners at the office and work on weekends. Often, this is by necessity. If a pitch is tomorrow and the work is not yet done, then it has to get done, period. As investment banking culture evolved, time spent at the office became a badge of honour, the distinct identity of the investment banker. From an office politics point-of-view, it can be *better* for a junior to take until 8 pm to finish a task than to have the same task finished in the same way by 6 pm. I never let anyone down by not completing a task and I never left the office before making sure there was no work left to do, but I had the reputation as a guy who didn't put in the hours. It made no objective sense, but the culture said otherwise. From the point-of-view of an interviewee, get ready to swim in this environment. Investment bankers are looking for a keener who will fit in. Even if you are not a keener/joiner type, think about presenting yourself in this way. If you are the complete opposite of a keener/joiner-type, think about not applying at all or applying to smaller, less conformist firms.

In my opinion (and as our anonymous friend above agrees), investment bankers are extremely concerned about their image of themselves as *investment bankers* – at times even to the detriment of monetary concerns. One example from my experience that springs to mind is a junior investment banker trying to impress a senior one by saying that "in my view, investment bankers are entrepreneurs." The observation was a bit strange. All three of us (senior, junior and myself) were employees of a 30,000+ person bank, in a 150+ professional department that relied on hundreds of legacy client relationships (including ones that sprang from lending, not investment banking, links) to generate business. None of us had started the bank or – I'm guessing a bit here, but I'm pretty sure – had any material amount of our net worth at risk in it. Key resources (e.g. the bank's retail broker network at the time of an IPO) had nothing to do with the investment banking department at all. As one of Canada's chartered banks, the bank itself had direct access (if needed) to the Bank of Canada (i.e. the guys who *print the money*) for advice, loans, whatever. I am still fond of the originator's remark, but what other 'entrepreneurs' operate in such circumstances?

This attitude is not new. In *Gentlemen of Fortune* (published 1984), Ferris writes, "Most investment bankers work for somebody else, although they tend to behave as if they didn't. They dislike being seen as the plodding servants of impersonal institutions." (p. 239) From the point of view of career choice and interviews, understand that investment bankers see themselves as very important and often as more important than, and independent from, many other related fields, e.g. corporate banking, retail broking, equity research. Can it all be too much? Yes, but know also that this investment banking *chutzpah* can be lots of fun. When you put in the hours and see the results (monetary and professional), being on the inside is very gratifying. One time in particular, coming home at 3 am after getting something done was very satisfying. As ever, be informed and choose investment banking if (on a net basis) it is a good career for you.

John Bridgman

Education:
BA, McGill University (1962)

Experience:
Research Analyst (Oil & Gas), Greenshields – Montreal (1962-68)

Senior Vice-President & Director (Investment Banking), Greenshields/Richardson Greenshields – Montreal (1968-94)

Investment Advisor & Director, Richardson Greenshields – Montreal (1994-95)

Investment Advisor & Vice-President, RBC Dominion Securities – Montreal (1995-99)

Director, Portfolio Manager, Member of Investment Policy Committee & Member of Executive Committee, MacDougall, MacDougall & MacTier – Montreal (1999-2004)

Current job:
Director, Portfolio Manager & Member of Investment Policy Committee, MacDougall, MacDougall & MacTier – Montreal (1999-)

How would you describe the function of an investment banker in the financial world? Why does this profession and set of responsibilities exist in this way?

"Historically, the role of 'investment banker' arose primarily in London, England. Investment bankers of the 17th and 18th centuries raised money for ventures. 'Raising money' could include a number of functions that have since become separate professions: being a middleman between providers and users of capital (the 'investment banking' of today), representing providers of capital on an ongoing basis (today's 'venture capitalist' or 'merchant banker') or providing (all or part of) the capital oneself (what today is often called 'commercial' or 'corporate' lending). The 'ventures' so financed could be a number of different things: geographic exploration and trade, shipping, financing goods, raising armies. Insurance was an adjunct to the investment banker's role in this era, as was spreading (through syndication) any risks that were assumed by a given party.

Eventually, the post-1929 Glass-Steagall Act in the United States (and equivalent legislation in Canada) separated the business of being a deposit-taking lender from being an underwriter of securities. Investment banking became very focussed on raising capital for companies through the issuance of securities (equity or debt) and on related advisory fields (especially M&A).

Now that Glass-Steagall and the equivalent legislation in Canada are no longer, investment banking at most firms is once again a part of a suite of services offered by integrated financial institutions, mainly banks. (Not all firms have gone that route: even though they are now publicly traded. Firms like Goldman Sachs and Lehman Brothers are still not deposit-taking institutions and are only involved in investment banking. Lazard remains both private and focussed entirely on investment banking.) Despite its less independent status, investment banking today remains a separate discipline: that of helping companies find capital as cheaply as possible, of related tasks (e.g. taking companies public, the sale of large blocks of shares) and of providing strategic advice about the use of that capital (especially M&A)."

How would you describe the job of an investment banker from a mechanical and day-to-day per-

spective?

"Let's take the case of a senior banker in the corporate finance field. The principal job of this professional is to find new business by marketing ideas to corporate clients. At meetings or on the phone, it is important to showcase the ability and capabilities of one's firm, but also to present ideas that can save the corporate client money or solve a financing need. Some ideas might revolve around saving a half point in interest; others might be about whole new ways to finance the project in question. Firms will divide up the market (sectorally, geographically etc …), but aside from that, the whole corporate universe is composed of potential clients. Within each target company all the key decision-makers (CEO, CFO, treasurer) have to be covered (i.e. kept informed and known personally) by the investment banking team. That is how deals are won."

What makes a good or bad investment banker?

"A good investment banker never stops thinking. As he shaves in the morning, he is thinking about what his first five calls will be. He has to be a good communicator and have good interpersonal skills. He has to be original and open-minded, otherwise new ideas will never get to market or will be exploited by the competition. He should like competition – and like having fun."

Who enjoys/dislikes investment banking?

"To enjoy investment banking you have to be flexible. You can't be a structured, 9-to-5 type. You have to be able to work long hours (including weekends) and move quickly from project to project – a multi-tasker. You have to be able to crunch numbers (computer literacy, especially regarding spreadsheets, is key) and think quickly without making mistakes. In the early years, get ready for a baptism of fire."

Investment banking in a sentence:
"It's not for the faint of heart or the thin-skinned or for anyone who dislikes competition – you have to like winning and want to make money."

Jean-François Marcoux

Education
Bachelor of Business Administration (Finance), HEC (University of Montreal) (1995)
MSc (Finance), University of Sherbrooke (1996)
Chartered Financial Analyst (CFA) designation, AIMR (2000)

Experience:
Associate (Global Markets), Deutsche Morgan Grenfell – Montreal (1996-98)
Analyst (Private Equity Investments in Telecommunications and Media), Capital Communications CDPQ (Caisse de dépôt et placement du Québec) – Montreal (1998-2000)
Associate Director (Investment Banking), Scotia Capital – Montreal (2000-03)

Current job:
Director (Mergers and Acquisitions), Transcontinental – Montreal (2003-)

How would you describe the function of an investment banker in the financial world? Why does this profession and set of responsibilities exist in this way?

"The investment banker is basically two things: a middle-man and a trusted financial advisor. The role of investment bankers consists of helping companies raise financing, whether through issuance of shares or debt, at the least dilutive price and at the best time. Investment bankers also act as mergers and acquisitions consultants to help companies identify, study, evaluate, negotiate and execute acquisitions. They also act as brokers to ensure the sale of companies or the divestiture of divisions. Investment bankers exist in this way because a middle-man often facilitates a buy/sell transaction (in the case of mergers and acquisitions) and because companies need to leverage the retail and institutional sales forces of investment banking firms to distribute and sell their shares or other financing instruments."

How would you describe the job of an investment banker from a mechanical and day-to-day perspective?
"There are two main aspects: prospecting mandates and execution of transactions. Prospecting mandates consists of finding creative financing or growth opportunities that may be available for a specific client. Various qualitative, strategic and financial analyses are frequently presented to clients (commonly called a client 'pitch') with the intention of eventually getting an execution mandate. Transaction execution consists of managing the entire transactional process: financial modeling and valuation, preparation of prospectuses and marketing documents, preparation of various presentations to investors, senior managers or boards of directors, negotiation of transaction terms and conditions, due diligence, communication and announcement of a transaction, etc ..."

What makes a good or bad investment banker?
"I believe that a good investment banker is one who can thoroughly listen to and, even more importantly, anticipate his client's needs. A good investment banker is also an individual with exceptional persuasive and people skills who can rationally bring various parties together to find benefits for themselves and reach an agreement. At a more junior level, a good banker is

someone who can easily summarize options, scenarios, alternatives and get to a recommendation."

Who enjoys or dislikes investment banking?

"Those who enjoy IB are those who do not mind being consultants, going from one mandate to another and living a very busy life with little time left for their families. Those who dislike IB are sometimes of an entrepreneurial nature and do not like to follow and lead processes. Introverted individuals also find it difficult evolving in IB. One must be crazy about finance and numbers to enjoy IB."

Investment banking in a sentence:

"IB is the art of finding a solution for any financing need or of finding ways to get a desirable acquisition done."

Job Ideas
Nota bene: Firms' locations should be used as a guide only. Toronto (or Montreal for firms that originated there) will be the office likely to hire the most people. Often some of the branch offices will be composed of one or two people in an individual field (investment banking, research etc …). Furthermore, firms tend to dislike people with geographic preferences. Nevertheless, if you want to be in a specific office, find out what goes on there and try to apply – or get there over time.

Key resource
Investment Dealers' Association of Canada www.ida.ca

The Bank-Owned
BMO Nesbitt Burns/Bank of Montreal (Toronto, Montreal, Vancouver, Calgary) www.nesbittburns.com
CIBC World Markets (Toronto, Montreal, Vancouver, Calgary, Ottawa) www.cibcwm.com
Desjardins Securities (Montreal) www.vmd.ca
Laurentian Bank Securities (Toronto, Montreal) www.vmbl.ca
National Bank Financial (Toronto, Montreal) www.nbfinancial.com
RBC Capital Markets/Royal Bank of Canada (Toronto, Montreal, Vancouver, Calgary, Regina, Ottawa, Halifax) www.rbccm.com
Scotia Capital/Bank of Nova Scotia (Toronto, Montreal, Vancouver, Calgary) www.scotiacapital.com
TD Securities (Toronto, Montreal, Vancouver, Calgary) www.tdsecurities.com

The Independents
Brant Securities (Toronto) www.brantsec.com
Canaccord (Toronto, Montreal, Calgary and Vancouver plus branches across Canada) www.canaccord.com

Casgrain & Company (Montreal) 514.871.8080
First Associates/Rockwater (Toronto) www.firstassociates.com
Genuity Capital Markets 416.603.6000
GMP Securities (Toronto, Montreal, Calgary)
   www.gmpsecurities.com
Haywood Securities (Vancouver, Calgary and Toronto)
   www.haywood.com
Loewen, Ondaatje, McCutcheon (Toronto) www.lomltd.com
Maison Placements (Toronto) www.maisonplacements.com
Northern Securities (Toronto, Vancouver and Calgary)
   www.northernsi.com
Orion (Toronto, Montreal and Calgary)
   www.orionsecurities.ca
Peters & Co. (Calgary) www.petersco.com
Research Capital (Toronto, Montreal, Calgary, Vancouver,
   plus branches across Ontario) www.researchcapital.com
Sprott Securities (Toronto, Montreal, Calgary) www.sprott.ca

The Foreign

Goldman Sachs (Toronto, Calgary) www.gs.com
JP Morgan (Toronto) www.jpmorgan.com
Lazard (Toronto, Montreal) www.lazard.com
Merrill Lynch (Toronto, Montreal, Vancouver, Calgary)
www.ml.com
Morgan Stanley (Toronto, Montreal)
www.morganstanley.com
N M Rothschild & Sons Canada Securities Limited (Toronto,
Montreal) 514.840.9560
Raymond James (Toronto and Vancouver)
www.raymondjames.ca
UBS (Toronto, Montreal, Vancouver, Calgary) www.ubs.com

2. Equity Analysis

Equity analysts (also called 'research analysts' or 'working in research') do research on the stocks of public companies and make recommendations about them to investor-clients.

From the point of view of the firm that hires the equity analysts, getting paid for the work of equity analysts is not an obvious proposition. In theory, the 'clients' of the equity analysts are the institutional investors (e.g. mutual and pension funds, investment counsellors, insurance companies etc ...) that trade the stocks that the firm covers. These investors indirectly pay for the research by executing trades with the firm's traders and paying commissions on the number of shares traded. Many of these investors have elaborate ranking criteria for analysts that determine how much commission revenue they will allocate to each analyst by trading with his firm. In fact, these commissions are often not enough to cover the payrolls of the trading and research departments in question.

As a result of this situation, there is a tendency for a firm's investment banking and research departments to be viewed jointly and as one cost/profit centre. Under this model, investment bankers and equity analysts work together to cover given companies. (One friend of mine went as far as describing his time as a *junior equity analyst* as working in 'banking', meaning investment banking.) The obvious problem is that the investment banking department has one client (the capital-raising company), the equity analyst has another (the fund that is buying or selling the stock on the analyst's recommendation) and the employer-firm has both. From the point of view of the investment banking department, however, the model is quite good. Investment banking, while increasingly industry-specific, is still more of a generic, skill-set oriented profession. Deals, companies and market darlings come and go, but the methods of raising capital do not change and investment bankers will always redeploy to the industry that is in vogue. Because equity analysts cover a limited number of stocks, 365 days a year, and often have operational expertise in their industry (see below), their knowledge tends to be more industry-specific. When it comes time to give a pitch for an investment banking mandate, the credibility that equity analysts provide can make the difference between getting the deal and losing it. From the point of view of the investment banking client, this model also works quite well. The investment bankers give technical, money-raising advice; the equity analysts cheerlead the company with the investing public and give industry-specific credibility to the marketing material of the investment banking department.

The picture is less rosy from the point of view of the client-investor and there have been some high profile problems with conflicts of interest under this model. Is the investor getting good advice from the equity analyst? Solutions are many: 'Chinese walls' forbidding communication between investment bankers and equity analysts, equity analysts being forced into silence as a new issue from an underwriting client approaches the market or even whole (albeit small) firms devoting themselves to research only. The pendulum has definitely swung against the equity-analyst-as-investment-banker model. One equity analyst friend explained to me that, while (at bonus time) he had once openly and explicitly touted the number of corporate finance deals he had worked on, doing so now (in 2004) would earn him time at a legal training seminar (or worse).

Regardless, it seems likely that equity analysis will remain a balancing act between clients with conflicting objectives and between employers trying to make as much money as possible on the investment banking side while not prostituting their research brand overmuch. No wonder one acquaintance of mine called equity analysis the hardest job on the street.

The day-to-day life of an equity analyst follows the public markets (9:30 am to 4 pm). Mornings start early with a review of new information regarding the market generally and the analyst's sector in particular. There will often be a morning meeting of the whole research staff to discuss any new issues of the day. From there, the analyst immerses himself in the business of covering his companies. There is an investigative, research aspect to this process: is this company good? do its plans make sense? is it worth $10 per share? is the multiple too rich? is it too much ahead or behind of its peers in terms of valuation? There is also a sales element. Formerly, analysts published material and institutional salesmen talked to clients to encourage them to buy or sell on the analysts' written recommendations. Clients became more and more interested in talking to the source of a given recommendation and less and less interested in reading the inches-thick pile of reports that came in daily by fax and internet. Getting the firm's analysts in touch with the fund managers became key to doing business (and, as the number of callers skyrocketed, increasingly difficult). An institutional salesman once described fund managers as "guys whose phones don't have any buttons" (i.e. they never call back). As a result, some firms now impose daily or weekly client call requirements on analysts. I once knew an analyst who told an institutional salesman that he didn't "do requests" (for reports or calls). He is no longer in the industry.

The analyst's job is especially busy as quarterly results are made public. This new, large block of quarterly information requires absorption by the analyst and his staff of juniors (often called 'associates') and makes the revision of the analyst's models, target prices and recommendations necessary. There is also a score-keeping aspect to the new information. For each given company, an analyst usually has a quarterly projection of revenue, EBITDA, EBIT, earnings, free cash flow etc … (which is either right or wrong or very wrong). (In addition, the analyst usually has forecasts for the next two years.) The analyst's success at predicting results (and the stock's direction) builds (or destroys) his credibility in the eyes of clients.

An analyst will usually cover 10 to 20 companies in a specific sector and have 1-2 associates. ('Analyst' is both a title and a job description. *The* analyst on a stock is the senior professional who has authorial credit and responsibility for the research. The 'associates' are the juniors who help him. From a job description point of view, both of them are 'equity analysts'. In addition to being an 'analyst', the senior professional may also have a rank, e.g. 'director', 'managing director' etc … To make things even more confusing, in investment banking, the pecking order is reversed: 'analyst' is often the rank of incoming BComm recruits and 'associate' is often the rank of MBA recruits.)

Often the analyst and the associates have operational experience or an educational background in their sector. The more specialized the field, the greater the likelihood that this will be the situation. For instance, the oil and gas and mining industries are fairly technical and experience in the field is worthwhile. On the high tech front, where 'gizmo' companies and ideas abound, technical expertise is also a big plus.

Culture

In my experience, the culture of equity analysts is a bit of a mix of the different cultures that I describe elsewhere in this book. When a deal (either underwriting or M&A) is done in their sector, they share the swagger of the investment banker – and, naturally enough and when possible, the quest for a piece of the profits. Their proximity to the trading function and to mutual fund or pension fund clients gives them some of the mental quickness and informality of the trader. At the same time, their 'deep research' function gives them a professorial air. They know (or ought to know) a lot about a given industry and the companies in it. They are not fly-by-night investment bankers who are on to the next deal before the ink is dry on today's, nor are they 'flip and forget' traders who might not revisit a stock for months. Their names will be on the next report about their sector, and the one after that. (This continuity of coverage can span several employers.) Like the job itself, the culture seems to be a balancing act between these forces.

Joseph Walewicz

Education:
BSc (Biochemistry), Queen's University (1992)
BA (Honours Economics), Queen's University (1993)
MBA, McGill University (1996)
CFA designation, AIMR (2000)

Experience:
Marketing Research Analyst, Pfizer Inc. – Montreal (1994-1996)
Research Associate (Biotechnology), Lehman Brothers – New York (1996-1997)
Research Analyst (Health Care & Biotechnology), Dlouhy Investments – Montreal (1997-2000)
Research Analyst (Biotechnology), BMO Nesbitt Burns – Montreal (2000-2003)

Current job:
Senior Health Care Analyst, Orion Securities – Montreal (2003-)

How would you describe the function of an equity analyst in the financial world? Why does this profession and set of responsibilities exist in this way?

"Research analysts have existed for decades. I think the reason is threefold. Firstly, having sell side research available to all buy siders is more efficient than funds doing all their own research. Large funds can (and do) have analysts dedicated by sector, but small funds simply can't afford that many researchers. A limited number of sell side analysts, on the other hand, can feed information to an infinite number of funds. Secondly, from the perspective of the buy side, there is never too much information or analysis. One portfolio manager will receive information and opinions from many analysts. As a result, he gets a very complete picture of a given sector. Thirdly, from the point of view of brokerage firms, offering research is a way to attract clients to a relatively undifferentiated service (stock trading) through a value-add product."

How would you describe the job of an equity analyst from a mechanical and day-to-day perspective?

"An analyst does three things: stays in touch with buy side clients, meets with companies that are being covered and generates research reports. An analyst will normally cover relatively few companies (10-15). Once these companies are under coverage, the research focus switches to maintenance research. You know the companies and the industry: it is just a question of staying up to date. In terms of generating research reports, the analyst is more of an editor, directing associates and editing the reports, with the ultimate responsibility for ratings and targets. While clients read the research, good reports must be combined with good stock picks and client service. Stock picking and constant communication with clients are the most important tasks."

What makes a good or bad equity analyst?

"Research is a service job with a strong emphasis on trust. A successful analyst is well ranked (and rewarded with trading business) by clients. A good ranking comes from making good calls on stocks and from keeping clients informed. One skill is not sufficient: a good stock picker who does not communicate frequently or effectively will not be successful in the industry. In terms of who is best qualified to pick stocks for a given sector, there has been a shift in the last 20 years away from analysts having purely financial backgrounds and towards individuals who come from industry. Knowing the sector from the inside is seen as a large plus. When I first joined the business, my boss told me that a good company, a good technology and a good stock are three different things, and never to mix them up. Investors and analysts often assume good companies are good stocks. There is no substitute for experience in this regard – good company research is the combination of number crunching and analysis, but good stock picking requires market savvy (gained from experience)."

Who enjoys or dislikes equity research?

"Research is a mixture of person-to-person marketing and pure analysis. If you are mainly interested in being a financial marketer, institutional sales is probably a better career for you. If you are only interested in crunching numbers, try corporate finance. Above and beyond that, all sorts of people should avoid research. For instance, if you dislike making cold calls; if you dislike investors and management teams being angry with you; or if you need to have your phone calls returned, then research will frustrate you. You also need to have a thick skin: when you make a bad call, investors will not let you forget. Conversely, good calls are rarely acknowledged (but appreciated, I think!). In general, no one *really* likes the analyst – but with good stock calls and good service you may get some clients to trust and respect you!"

Equity research in a sentence:
  "If you've got thick skin coated with Teflon, this is a job for you."

Philippe Marleau

Education:
Bachelor of Engineering, Major in Civil Engineering with Minor in Economics, McGill University (1996)
CFA designation, AIMR (1999)

Experience:
Investor Relations, Ste-Genevieve Resources Ltd. – Toronto (1996-1997)
Associate (real estate equity research), Scotia Capital Inc. – Toronto (1997-2000)
Vice-President (gaming & lodging equity research), Merrill Lynch Inc. – New York City (2000-2004)

Current job:
Principal, MVEST Management, LLC (Hedge Fund) – New York City (2004-)

How would you describe the function of an equity analyst in the financial world? Why does this profession and set of responsibilities exist in this way?

"The primary function of an equity analyst is to provide investment advice and recommendations on specific stocks within an industry to institutional investors such as mutual funds and pension funds. This profession exists in this way because most mutual funds and pension funds do not have the resources to follow individual stocks to the level of depth that an industry expert would. These institutions pay for this industry expertise and research via brokerage commissions."

How would you describe the job of an equity analyst from a mechanical and day-to-day perspective?

"An equity analyst starts his/her day by scanning the

newswires for anything pertaining to their sector of coverage. If something important has occurred in their sector, they provide a quick summary and analysis for their clients. For a large part of the day, the analyst is conducting company and industry studies, analyzing company financials, maintaining financial models, and talking to corporate and operating management as well as industry contacts in an effort to uncover investment ideas or reinforce their stance on a stock. The analyst will usually present their findings to the sales force at one of the firm's morning meetings and follow up with clients through phone conversations. At the end of the day, the analyst brings several industry publications home, to keep up with the most recent developments in their field."

What makes a good or bad equity analyst?

"A good analyst is creative, has very strong analytical skills and excellent communication skills (both verbal and written). The best analysts can continually come up with original research, possess a vast amount of industry knowledge, can think independently and objectively, and have some level of salesmanship."

Who enjoys or dislikes equity analysis?

"People who have a strong appreciation for the stock market, have a desire to become an expert in a specific field, enjoy picking stocks, and like to 'sell' their investment ideas will enjoy equity research."

In a sentence:

"An equity analyst gets paid to discover investment ideas."

Job Ideas

Nota bene: Firms' locations should be used as a guide only. Toronto (or Montreal for firms that originated there) will be the office likely to hire the most people. Often some of the branch offices will be composed of one or two people in an individual field (investment banking, research etc ...). Furthermore, firms tend to dislike people with geographic preferences. Nevertheless, if you want to be in a specific office, find out what goes on there and try to apply – or get there over time.

Key resource
Investment Dealers' Association of Canada www.ida.ca

The Bank-Owned
BMO Nesbitt Burns (Bank of Montreal) www.nesbittburns.com
CIBC World Markets www.cibcwm.com
Desjardins Securities (Montreal) www.vmd.ca
Laurentian Bank Securities www.vmbl.ca
National Bank Financial www.nbfinancial.com
RBC Capital Markets (Royal Bank of Canada) www.rbccm.com
Scotia Capital (Bank of Nova Scotia) www.scotiacapital.com
TD Securities www.tdsecurities.com

The Independents
Brant Securities (Toronto) www.brantsec.com
Canaccord (Toronto, Montreal, Calgary and Vancouver plus branches across Canada) www.canaccord.com
Casgrain & Company (Montral) 514.871.8080
First Associates/Rockwater (Toronto) www.firstassociates.com
GMP Securities (Toronto, Montreal and Calgary)

www.gmpsecurities.com
Haywood Securities (Vancouver, Calgary and Toronto)
www.haywood.com
Loewen, Ondaatje, McCutcheon (Toronto) www.lomltd.com
Maison Placements (Toronto) www.maisonplacements.com
Northern Securities (Toronto, Vancouver and Calgary)
www.northernsi.com
Orion (Toronto, Montreal and Calgary)
www.orionsecurities.ca
Peters & Co. (Calgary) www.petersco.com
Research Capital (Toronto, Montreal, Calgary and Vancouver plus branches across Ontario) www.researchcapital.com
Sprott Securities (Toronto, Montreal and Calgary)
www.sprott.ca

The Foreign
Raymond James (Toronto and Vancouver)
   www.raymondjames.ca
UBS www.ubs.com
Merrill Lynch www.ml.com

3. Lending (Corporate Banking)

Lending does not really belong in the sell side section. Unlike the 'true' sell side disciplines, lenders do not set out to fulfil/analyze a corporate need for money and then meet it by tapping/advising the capital markets. They lend and leave the loan (or a part of it) on their balance sheet. Nevertheless, the degree of integration between investment and corporate banking (see "A Note on 'Integration'", below) led me to include it in this section.

Corporate bankers lend their employers' money to companies. 'Corporate' banking is the usual term used to describe lending at a high dollar threshold, e.g. $20-30+ million at one time. ('Commercial' banking applies to the dollar bracket underneath 'corporate'. To make things confusing, in some jurisdictions, 'commercial banking' means the business of lending money, period, and is used to distinguish *all lending* from, say, *investment* banking.) In Canada, this field is undoubtedly dominated by the 'big five' banks (Bank of Montreal/BMO, CIBC, Royal/RBC, TD, Scotia) and the other major Schedule I banks (National and to a lesser extent, Laurentian and Canadian Western Bank), although other players (Schedule II – i.e. foreign – banks, Quebec's Caisse de Dépôt et Placement, GE Capital, Teachers, Congress) are in the market for some lending products, especially senior debt (see below).

Corporate lending includes two principal products: senior debt and operating lines (also called 'revolvers', although this second term can apply more narrowly to a hybrid product that is a cross between an operating line and senior debt). Senior debt is a loan of a certain amount of money extended by a bank to a company. The loan will have an interest rate (fixed or floating), a term (at the end of which any remaining principal is due), a principal repayment schedule (to reduce the principal during the term of the loan) and covenants.

Covenants are financial ratios (e.g. debt / EBITDA, EBITDA / fixed obligations) that the company pledges to keep above or below certain thresholds. Often the thresholds become more difficult to meet as the loan progresses – although company growth and debt repayment *should* make meeting them feasible. The two numbers in a given ratio are usually made up of numbers representing loan obligations (e.g. interest, principal outstanding or principal repayment obligations) on one hand and numbers representing company performance (EBITDA, EBIT, free cash flow) on the other. The idea behind stricter covenant thresholds over time is that the company should have grown in the intervening years and that the loan obligations should have been reduced. (In every lending agreement, there are also many covenants limiting the amount of – or requiring consent for – capital expenditures, asset sales, leasing etc … but these are more standard across lending agreements and do not get companies into trouble – or negotiation – as often as the financial covenants.)

If financial covenants have not been met, the corporate banker is alerted that something is wrong and perhaps something should be done. The banker's options at this point are numerous and range in severity from trifling to harsh: waive the covenant in question for the violation period (either in return for money or *gratis*), require partial repayment of the loan (through an equity injection or the borrowing of new debt subordinated to the bank's loan), restructure the loan (i.e. basically loan money on entirely new and worse terms to retire the old loan), insist on changes in the company's operations (e.g. asset sales), install some sort of bank representative (receiver etc ...) to represent the bank's interest until the covenants are again onside or, apocalyptically, call the loan whatever the consequences, including bankruptcy proceedings. The bank and banker must tread a line between being overly harsh (and so alienating the borrower in question and perhaps, by word of mouth, other possible clients) and being overly generous (and so perhaps losing an opportunity to salvage the bank's money while the going is still good).

From the point of view of the client, the lower the interest rate, the longer the term, the less onerous the principal repayments, the better. Counter-intuitively, for many clients, the interest rate is less important than the loan's terms (repayment schedule, term, covenants). Why? The interest rate can eat into an equity holder's returns, true, but a percentage point or two of interest does not make that much difference. Not meeting conditions in a loan agreement, however, puts a company in default and out of the driver's seat. Default can effectively bankrupt a company or put it into costly and time-consuming negotiations with its incumbent or replacement bankers. From the point of view of the bank, however, the shorter the term and the faster the principal repayments, the less risk and the more control they have. (Regulated banks also have incentives to lend shorter term due to their need to meet certain loan/capital ratios. Longer terms loans eat up room in these regulatory ratios more than shorter term ones.)

Senior debt is usually disbursed in large amounts at one time. The 'papering' and negotiation of these loans takes up a lot of time and money. A typical moment would be when one company buys another (and borrows money to do so) or when a private equity firm buys a portfolio company (and borrows money inside the portfolio company to do so) or when there is a large capital project that a company wants to finance with new debt or when existing debt is re-financed.

An operating line is a facility extended by a bank to a company that allows it to borrow up to a certain dollar amount on an as-needed basis. In addition to being a part of the company's 'debt' for senior facility ratio calculation purposes and in addition to the total limit of the facility, there is often a specific, ratio-defined limit to borrowing under an operating line. This limit is usually a percentage of accounts receivable and inventory. While the presence, absence and extent of senior debt varies greatly among even public companies (from overleveraged to massive net cash balances), most companies will have an operating line "just in case." The required amount of the operating line will, however, vary greatly between companies. Very seasonal companies (e.g. retail, manufacturers of summer or winter products) will require much larger operating lines than more seasonally stable ones (e.g. auto parts, printing). Manufacturing businesses that build up inventory and receivables before in fact getting paid are more likely to need (and get) large operating lines, versus service business that have no inventory to finance and should be paid regularly (and so have no receivables 'bulge' at a given time in the year).

Large loans (senior and operating) tend to be syndicated. The larger the loan, the greater the likelihood of syndication. Syndication is simply the process of bringing in other banks to lend some of the money and so share the risk. The lead bank captains the negotiation with the borrower, liaises with other banks, represents the syndicate vis-à-vis the borrower on a going-forward basis and benefits economically from being the lead. The other syndicate members are not silent partners, however, and can have quite disparate views on how to deal with a given client's non-compliance with covenants. These views have traction due to the contractual lending agreement through which they can demand repayment etc ...

The day-to-day life of a corporate banker is focussed on monitoring existing loans and pursuing new ones. Monitoring existing loans requires watching the ratios discussed above and keeping in touch with clients about their business' ups and downs. Change can mean trouble or new opportunities for lending. Pursuing new deals means understanding the company in question, assessing its needs and working on putting together a winning term sheet. Even then, the deal in question must be approved by the bank's credit department. This internal division of the bank is not well understood by outsiders. The public face of the bank (the corporate banker) does not have the power to lend. He is a deal maker intent on getting the business in question. More lending means that he has sold more of his 'product' and put more of the bank's money to work. He cares about the viability of the borrower, but not enough to be allowed free rein. The banks have instituted a check on this more sales-oriented role by requiring that loans go through a 'credit department' before being approved. Credit employees are more conservative than the corporate bankers (and are differently compensated). They look at the downside of the proposed deal and at the bank's overall exposure to the industry or risk factors in question.

Culture

If I had to summarize the corporate bankers I've met, I'd say 'sceptical'. When the music stops, it is most often the lenders that are left holding the bag. Take the case of a failed LBO (leveraged buyout). The investment bankers who advised the seller of the company in question and those who advised the buyer will have been paid their commission long since. The merchant bankers who sponsored the deal can make up the losses from one equity investment with the better than expected profits of another. Any traders dealing with the company (fx, commodities, etc ...) will usually have a minimal exposure. Trades either settle or they don't. Even if they don't, the exposure can end up in a gain. Lenders, however, get to tour all the ravaged battlefields: the straight bankruptcies, the workouts, the re-financings. Their capital is at risk until it is paid off, period. They cannot make up losses on one deal with spectacular gains on another because their returns are capped by an interest rate. That rate may be variable, but it will never generate returns like equity. The bankers have been caught several times. Repeated third world meltdowns. Overleveraging in the 1980's. The dot.coms, telecom boom and financial engineering of the 1990's. Repeated real estate debacles. Their upside is limited, but they can lose their whole investment. Can you blame their lack of enthusiasm for adventurism?

> **Pierre Matuszewski**
>
> **Education:**
> BA (Economics), Université Laval (1977)
> MBA, McGill University (1979)
>
> **Experience:**
> Executive Vice President & Member of the Executive Committee, Scotia McLeod Inc. – Montreal (1979-90)
> Advisor to Senior Management/Executive Vice President, National Bank/Lévesque Beaubien Geoffrion – Montreal (1990-92)
> Vice President, Treasurer and Member of Management Group, Laurentian Group Corporation – Montreal (1992-94)
> Director (Investment Banking), Richardson Greenshields – Montreal (1994-96)
>
> **Current job:**
> Managing Director and Head of Corporate & Investment Banking, SG Canada – Montreal (1996-)

How would you describe the function of a corporate banker in the financial world? Why does this profession and set of responsibilities exist in this way?

"Firstly, from the point of view of the client-company, bank loans are the initial layer, and a prime source of, credit. While credit exists as a capital markets product (via publicly issued bonds), this avenue is not open to all companies: some have needs that are too small to justify a bond issue, some are too risky for the market's taste and some do not have the public profile for a bond issue. In addition, having a single lender can be a big advantage for the borrower. If anything needs changing (e.g. term, covenants, amounts), dealing with one bank (or one syndicate) is much easier than amending the terms of a publicly issued bond.

From the point of view of financial firms, lending is an 'anchor' product. In recent years, banks have grown in size and declined in number. Lending is a product that is in demand in its own right and that opens doors for the other products that these larger, more complex banks offer. Why can lending open doors? Lending implies trust. In order to lend money, a lender must know and trust the borrower and *vice versa*. If the bank trusts the client, it will be willing (and keen) to take on risks in regards to that client. If a client trusts the lending bank, the client will seek out the bank's advice on all sorts of financial problems and opportunities. Corporate bankers are thus a key pipeline to sell other non-credit products: structured financings, debt underwriting, equity underwriting and other types of advice."

How would you describe the job of a corporate banker from a mechanical and day-to-day perspective?

"There are four major parts to the job. Firstly, there is a coordination function. The corporate banker is often the guardian of client relationships and knows where a client's entry points are for different types of decisions. The bank's efforts to service the client will thus go through the corporate banker. Secondly, there is a processing function. As a bank tailors a given product for a client, the corporate banker's views are key: is the product right for the client? Is the risk right for the bank? A long term lending relationship gives the banker insight into these questions. Thirdly, there is deal execution. In the field of lending, the corporate banker is the bank's expert professional. Potential deals come from many sources (e.g. from the client, from the bank itself, from external events), but each one must be won and executed properly. Winning deals means pitching to clients and potential clients, and finding the right price for a given risk. 'Execution' includes a variety of tasks, including due diligence, documenting the transaction properly and internal communication. One of the differences between investment banking and corporate banking is the amount of work that must be done with your own credit department to sell a given deal *internally*. Fourthly, there is a more general 'thinking' function. The goal of the banker is to be viewed as a trusted advisor by the client. The objective is to be the person whom the client calls when he has a problem or opportunity."

What makes a good or bad corporate banker?
"A good corporate banker has empathy with clients, is a good salesman and understands the products he is selling. People often lose sight of salesmanship. Having an MBA is not enough: in order to win deals you have to be a salesman at heart. Understanding products is also important, although in the large complex banks of today one person might be responsible for selling 30 products. You can't be an expert in all of them, but you've got to have a good feel for each.

On the client side, you have to understand the rhythm of a company. There is a time for pitching certain ideas and a time not to. Some ideas can be executed quickly, although in this world of increased corporate governance, those same ideas (e.g. complex derivative products) may have to be explained in some detail to the client's entire board of directors before being allowed to proceed. In one case at our bank, extensive modelling and data were required as part of the decision-making process. We did the deal, but assembling all of the information took two years. You have to understand the time required and be patient.

On a more personal level, while you have to be hungry for business, you've got to be a team player both internally and vis-à-vis your clients. You should have an ego, but also be humble. I find being successful and involved in other activities – professionally, intellectually or as a hobby – helps with your career: it makes you an *interesting person* for the client to interact with."

Who enjoys or dislikes corporate banking?

"You have to be patient. Corporate banking is very different from selling bonds or being a retail salesman. There is not that instant gratification. There is a ramp-up period to doing a deal, somewhat like the time a leopard spends stalking its prey. If you like that strategic aspect, this might be the field for you. Corporate banking is also very different from a research or consulting job where the analysis continues at a relatively constant pace. In both investment and corporate banking, there is the build up to a climactic closing. You've got to enjoy that kind of work and delayed pay-off to enjoy this job."

Corporate banking in brief:

"Money is the ultimate store of value and means of exchange for businesses. Corporate banking is the 99-balls-in-the-air profession that supervises the flow of that commodity."

Marc-André Aubé

Education:
Ing., École Polytechnique, (University of Montreal) (1995)
MBA, HEC (University of Montreal) (1999)
CFA designation, AIMR (2002)

Experience:
Associate (Corporate Banking), Bank of Nova Scotia – Montreal (1999-2003)

Current job:
Financial Analyst (Corporate Debt), CDP Capital Amérique (Caisse de dépôt et placement du Québec) – Montreal
Part time: MBA Lecturer, HEC (University of Montreal) – Montreal

How would you describe the function of a corporate banker in the financial world?

"The role of a corporate banker is to assess the risk of transactions in order to properly adjust the return (interest rate) that will be asked of a given customer. This rate needs to be attractive enough to win business while still covering the loan loss probability.

A good corporate banker needs to maintain excellent relationships with his current customers (as well as prospective ones) since the best deals rarely come knocking. You need to fight to win deals and fight to deserve to get them. Poor business development skills will lead to a corporate banker or bank only being solicited to participate in deals that are less popular in the marketplace and this development could translate into higher loan losses over time."

Why does this profession and set of responsibilities exist in this way?

"Companies need money to expand and develop. The new projects will create value if they answer a need in the population and people are ready to pay for the new or improved services. The loan will then be paid down by the liquidity generated from the project. The spread between the risk-free interest rate and the rate charged pays for the general expenses of the corporate banking team, covers the loan loss provisions and provides a decent return on the capital employed by the lending institution."

How would you describe the job of a corporate banker from a mechanical and day-to-day perspective?

"The day-to-day tasks of the corporate banker can be split in three:

First, loan portfolio management. This task includes following the results of the companies to which you lend. The goal is to assess as quickly as possible any under-performance that could trigger the financial covenants that companies need to meet and to assess the financial flexibility of your clients so that you can be ready to offer additional funds when the need arises. At most institutions, a yearly document needs to be prepared to communicate to the organization the banker's evaluation of all the companies under management. This process is called the annual review.

Secondly, business development activities. Deals typically do not fall into your lap. A good corporate banker needs to generate ideas for his clients and prospects in order to win business. Corporate bankers have to obtain meetings with companies, write PowerPoint 'pitchbooks' explaining transaction ideas (M&A, refinancing and others) and present them with professionalism. Business development includes lunch seminars, smaller lunch meetings and *cinq-à-septs* (cocktails) with other banks, clients and prospects.

Thirdly, transaction management. When you get a deal, you need to negotiate the details of the transaction, perform your due diligence and, finally, agree on the legal documentation. Typically, there can be 3-6 new deals per year and 2-3 refinancings of existing customers."

What makes a good or bad corporate banker?

"Good corporate bankers can properly assess risk and have good technical/analytical skills, while still being able to sell ideas. Ultimately, a good corporate banker will generate new transactions while losing less than the average loan loss of the market.

Note: typically, the loan loss probability for first rank loans is in the 1% to 3% range. This means that an average portfolio will lose between 1 and 3% of its portfolio value per year, on average, over a long period. Loan losses tend to be concentrated in some years and in some industries."

Who enjoys or dislikes corporate banking?

"Someone who is a curious, self-driven person and who likes a mix of analytical and business development activities will enjoy corporate banking. People that are not comfortable with stress and tight deadlines or that cannot work in a serious environment that must (at times) be inflexible will not like this kind of job."

Corporate banking in brief:
"Philosophically speaking, the corporate banker is the gatekeeper who directs capital towards those parts of the economy where it is most needed (read: where it will generate more cash flow). Corporate banking allows you to create value while understanding where economic activity is taking place."

Job Ideas

Nota bene: Firms' locations should be used as a guide only. Toronto (or Montreal for firms that originated there) will be the office likely to hire the most people. Often some of the branch offices will be composed of one or two people in an individual field (investment banking, research etc ...). Furthermore, firms tend to dislike people with geographic preferences. Nevertheless, if you want to be in a specific office, find out what goes on there and try to apply – or get there over time.

Key resource
The Office of the Superintendent of Financial Institutions (OSFI) www.osfi-bsif.gc.ca

Schedule I et al.
Bank of Montreal/BMO www.nesbittburns.com or www4.bmo.com
Bank of Nova Scotia/Scotia Bank www.scotiacapital.com or www.scotiabank.com/
Canadian Western Bank www.cwbank.com
CIBC www.cibcwm.com or www.cibc.com
Desjardins www.vmd.ca or www.desjardins.com
Laurentian Bank www.vmbl.ca or www.laurentianbank.com
National Bank www.nbfinancial.com or www.nbc.ca
Royal Bank of Canada/RBC www.rbccm.com or www.rbc.com
TD www.tdsecurities.com or www.td.com

Schedule II
BNP Paribas (Canada) (Montreal, Quebec City, Toronto, Vancouver) www.bnpparibas.ca
Citibank Canada (Toronto, Montreal, Calgary, London and Vancouver) www.citibank.com/canada

HSBC Bank Canada (offices throughout Canada) www.hsbc.ca
J.P. Morgan Canada (Toronto) www.jpmorgan.com
Société Générale (Canada) (Montreal, Toronto, Quebec, Winnipeg) www.sgcib.com
UBS Bank (Canada) (Toronto, Montreal, Vancouver, Calgary) www.ubs.com

Other
Caisse/Caisse de dépôt et placement du Québec (Montreal, Quebec City) www.lacaisse.com
Teachers (Toronto) www.otpp.com
GE Capital (offices throughout Canada) www.gecapitalcanada.com
Congress Financial of Canada/Wachovia (Toronto, Montreal, Vancouver) www.congressfinancial.com

A Note on 'Integration'

In Canada, the Charter I banks (Bank of Montreal/BMO, CIBC, Royal/RBC, TD, Scotia, National, Laurentian and Canadian Western Bank) used to be forbidden from owning investment dealers (back in the day, Wood Gundy, Dominion Securities, McLeod Young Weir, Nesbitt Thomson, Burns Fry, First Marathon, Gordon Capital etc ...) that underwrote publicly traded securities and employed retail brokers. In the late 1980's and early 1990's, this prohibition was lifted and 4 of the 5 major banks (Bank of Montreal/BMO, CIBC, Royal/RBC, Scotia) bought the major investment dealers (respectively, Nesbitt Thompson/Burns Fry, Wood Gundy, Dominion Securities, McLeod Young Weir) and began integrating them into their operations.

This process did not take place overnight. Obvious redundancies (e.g. two economics departments) went first. Then physical offices were streamlined. From the point of view of this section, the most important phase was the last one and involved integrating the newly acquired 'investment bank' (i.e. underwriting and M&A) with the 'corporate bank' (i.e. lending) at a personnel level. Basically, the banks wanted to be able to go to a client-company with one person (or team) and offer all of their products (i.e. lending, raising equity, raising debt, securitization, plus other more technical products, e.g. cash management) through that one point of contact. This meant fusing the client relations efforts of the two banks (investment and corporate) and, to some extent, the cultures as well. (At least the point of contact would have to know both investment banking and corporate banking products.)

The task was not easy! Investment bankers are glory boys. They are more aggressive, tend be more mobile between jobs, are higher paid and work longer hours. Corporate bankers are more conservative (even though it is the credit department that is the ultimate guardian of the bank's capital), less likely to move between jobs and are paid less. (Regarding job mobility, remember that some investment banking services – e.g. M&A, securitization – *require no capital whatsoever* and most others (e.g. underwriting) require capital that turns over very quickly – or should. As a result, there is always the possibility of starting a boutique investment banking shop – and experience to date has borne this out. Try starting a boutique chartered or corporate bank.)

In any event, the task of integration is now largely done at the chartered banks. The point of contact is usually called a 'relationship manager' and is responsible for retailing all the bank's company-oriented products. At the lower levels, the juniors still work in their functional 'silo' (e.g. investment banking, corporate banking), but already the junior must have a greater awareness of the bank's other products than 5, 10 or 15 years ago, and this requirement increases as the junior moves up the corporate ladder. (In addition to organizing the staff into functional silos that back up the relationship manager, some banks also organize these same 'functional' people into industry groups that cut across silos. The result is a 'matrix' structure where each junior has a functional superior and an industry superior.)

Section III. The Buy Side

The buy side is so called because participants have the money (or represent people who have the money) to buy the products dreamed up by the sell side. The atmosphere is less frenzied in this area of finance. Moves of professionals and clients between firms are less frequent. Buy side professional will take the time to assess deals and will often pass. Unlike sell side professionals who, as agents, are on to the next deal when a given one closes, buy siders may have to live with the deals or stocks that they buy into for years to come.

It is important to remember that buy siders have another whole aspect to their business: interaction with their clients, the real owners of the money they invest. This relationship may be one-on-one (e.g. for a retail broker) or may be arm's length (e.g. the relationship of a pension fund manager with the fund's thousands of beneficiaries). Financial results matter, but so do client relations. Sometimes accounts can be kept even in the face of below average performance.

4. Retail Broking

Retail brokers buy and sell the stocks of public companies for clients. (Retail brokers are also called 'salesmen', 'registered representatives', 'account executives', 'investment representative' and 'investment advisors'.) They can also buy and sell bonds, money market instruments (t-bills, bankers' acceptances, commercial paper) and mutual funds. Their clients tend to be individuals, although some retail brokers will also cover institutional clients (i.e. money that is managed through investment management firms, pension funds and mutual funds).

Of all the professions covered in this book, retail broking has probably changed the least in the last 100 years. (Some of the professions covered here – e.g. venture capital, merchant banking, mezzanine lending – didn't even exist 50 years ago.) Their clients are actual people with whom they communicate by telephone or in person. Technology, de-/re-regulation and advances in portfolio management have affected the business' speed, overall context (many brokers now work indirectly for the chartered banks) and vocabulary, but an unsophisticated client who signed up with a broker in 1955 and stayed with him until now would find many aspects of service unchanged.

The retail broker's job is to recommend stocks to his clients and execute these solicited trades, plus any unsolicited ones. Although the content of the advice is important, building a retail 'book' (i.e. of clients) depends more on the *manner* of service than the *content* – within reason. Retail brokers find clients among their existing friends and family, socially, through contacts, through cold calls and, to a lesser extent, through their firm. Because of the personal relationship between the broker and the client and the fact that retail clients are trusting their own money to the broker, the level of service is higher, more frequent and more personal than most of the 'wholesale' businesses covered in this book.

Due to the possible (and frequent) interaction between the broker and completely unsophisticated members of the public, the profession has attracted more and more regulation over the years and is likely to continue to do so. Brokers must pass exams (the Canadian Securities Course, and the Conduct and Practices Handbook Course) and be licensed before they can deal with the public. One of the cardinal rules of this training is the 'know your client' rule. Brokers should know a lot about their clients' financial situation and goals. All investment advice should be given through the prism of these constraints.

Traditionally, brokers have been relatively free agents within their employer firms. Indeed, many firms of the past were structured (in spirit, if not legally) as partnerships of brokers. Broker A might have been recommending the purchase of Stock A, while in the next office, Broker B was advising the sale of Stock A and the purchase of Stock B. In the past, the amount of research and stock picking done by the individual brokers was greater (or could be – depending on the broker's preference). The evolution of financial theory, of research techniques and of the need for firms to limit their exposure to lawsuits etc … has changed this situation. Many firms will have a model portfolio (or stock by stock research) created by a dedicated research team that brokers use to build individual portfolios. Under this business model, the broker's job becomes more one of applying and explaining existing research than of actually making decisions about stocks.

Brokers are often quite independent from their employer firms and really act as entrepreneurs. Some of the rookie investment bankers I worked with were shocked to learn from the syndication desk (where new issues of stock or debt are finally sold to buyers) that 'our' bank's brokers would not automatically mouth the party line given to them by the investment banking department. The regulators would have been pleased. The brokers in this example were loyal to their true clients, not their nominal employer. The clients – in fact if not in theory – belong to the brokers. They (and their assistants) are often the only interaction that the client has with the firm. Brokers can (and do) move around between firms and bring clients with them. The loyalty of clients to individual brokers and the ability of retail firms to exist without vast capital reserves keep the extent of firm control in check. (In the mid-1990's, one of the bank-owned firms purchased an independent brokerage firm. The 'acquired' brokers had been working on a Windows-based system, but the buyer's brokers were still using DOS-based systems. The acquiring firm forced the 'acquired' brokers to *go back* to DOS. The remaining independents picked up some brokers in the ensuing period.)

Despite the lack of radical change in the day-to-day life of the profession, there are major threats to the retail broker's business. In the lower net worth market, the advent of mutual funds and of discount broking has eaten into the potential customer base. If you wanted to invest in 1960, you invested with a broker. If you want to invest now, you can invest directly in a mutual fund or buy and sell stocks yourself by opening a discount brokerage account. In the high net worth marketplace, individuals can opt for an investment manager who will manage the whole account for a fee.

Some retail brokers have responded to this last threat by becoming, in effect or in fact, investment managers. In addition or instead of per trade commissions, they charge a fee based on the amount of wealth managed and they seek out accreditation to be able to manage accounts. The only difference is that their firms have the ability to execute trades in-house. This development has 'created' (it existed in the past as well) a regulatory issue (some brokers control the number of trades and get paid per trade).

One important point to recall about retail broking: if you start your career right out of school without a 'book' to inherit or take over, it will be a long, uphill battle to build a viable base of clients. The firms have trainee programs and give individuals time to prove their worth, but the challenge and threat is there from day one. Most people can make some headway with friends and family, but eventually it comes down to cold calls and hours of prospecting work.

Retail broking has a bad reputation in some circles. The public can see brokers as bucket shop operators. Among other professionals, retail broking does not always have a reputation for intelligence and industry knowledge. A seasoned market player once told me, "Maybe so-and-so was an institutional salesman and so doesn't understand investment banking. Or maybe she was a retail broker – and *they* don't know *anything*." I can't agree. I've found retail brokers to be as smart as the other groups I've been exposed to and working in as viable a profession as the others I know of. If the best revenge is to live a long life, I've witnessed the retail brokers avenge themselves. When I was being trained by one of the chartered banks to be an investment banker, it arranged for all the various trainees (investment and corporate bankers, traders etc ...) to attend presentations from various branches of the firm. For all sorts of reasons (pay, hours, freedom), the one presentation that made this very confident group of people sit up, take notice and maybe questions their career path was retail broking. For those whose careers work out, it can be a great profession: financially rewarding, boss-free (or at least light) and fun.

Culture
Retail broking is a sales-oriented profession. You can be as smart as a whip, but if you have no clients, you will have no business. For this reason, retail brokers are outgoing, self-confident and gregarious. In my experience, retail brokers, despite the similarity of their job to money management, are much less formal and more irreverent. Maybe their (historic) proximity to the trading pits has kept them from being too earnest. On the investment side, they take pride in picking winners and avoiding losers – sometimes ostentatiously. There was one broker I knew who had a little victory ritual when he sold a stock at a profit. At the time, one of the newspapers had a personalized mass mail-out that sent prospective customers a fake headline with their name in it that read, "John Smith Triumphs Again". Part of this broker's victory dance involved flipping these signs (with his name on them) into view and doing a Nixon-style double victory salute. I can't imagine a money manager doing that, but this broker did it once every month or so.

Richard Hart

Education:
BA, McGill University (1965)

Experience:
Investment advisor, Greenshields/Richardson Greenshields (1965-90)
Investment advisor, Thompson Kernaghan (1990-2003)

Current job:
Investment advisor, MacDougall, MacDougall & MacTier (2003-)

How would you describe the function of a retail broker in the financial world? Why does this profession and set of responsibilities exist in this way?

"The way I interpret the job of a broker is slightly different from others. My idea of a broker encompasses more than just someone who buys and sells stocks and bonds upon the request of a client. In the past, most brokers were order takers – those days are long gone. Brokers were not unlike used car salesmen: the investment firm told them what to buy or sell depending on what the research department was recommending or on what inventory was left on the shelf from the last investment banking deal. (One can sense a certain creeping cynicism from years of being witness to these less than ethical methods.) Now, a broker must consider the client's objectives, time horizons and ability to accept risk. Heavy compliance departments oversee everything a broker does. He must be an all-around investment advisor and portfolio manager who can detect the smallest unwritten sensibility in achieving financial success and peace of mind for the client.

An ethical broker is a great value proposition today. The problem is people get confused and driven away from their financial objectives by fancy terms and complicated propositions that don't make any sense. Consider mutual funds – they are expensive, averaging a yearly fee of 2.6% in Canada, and have been poor performers. Consider wrap accounts, sold largely by bank-driven investment firms that charge 1–3% annually and give you the opportunity of having your portfolio managed by a professional 'third party'. A typical wrap account looks like someone has taken 5 shares of every stock listed on the market and placed it in the account. Everyone along this food chain – i.e., broker, the 'professional' money manager and the investment house must be paid. That is why the fee is so high! How can your portfolio perform when you start with that sort of deficit every year? This is the problem: they don't perform."

How would you describe the job of a retail broker from a mechanical and day-to-day perspective?
"The first thing the successful broker must do is become his own private investigator of financial information: he must review the major newspapers every day, after which (between 8:45 – 9:30 pm), he will set up the trades that have been agreed upon since the previous day's closing. In my situation, from about 9 am until after I have left the office (around 6 pm), the phone doesn't stop. Communication is perpetual and very necessary. E-mails take second seat to the phone and sometimes won't be seen for awhile – most of my clients know that if they e-mail me, they should copy my assistant to ensure it will be seen in a timely fashion. Once, and very often twice, a month, I spend time

at night or on a weekend away from the phone, computer and office reviewing the hard-copy portfolios of all my accounts. People in the industry kid me about this paper-based approach, but it is the only way I have found to be on top of what has happened in an account over a short period and especially events over which I have had no influence (i.e., cash in and cash out, dividends, interest payments etc …). In addition to all of this, I am thinking about the stock market all the time and what I should be advising clients. I try to spot trends, develop strategies, study all types of research whether it be in-house or outside research, look for ideas (the life blood of the industry) and, most importantly, I discuss all this with a network across the country of colleagues built up over 40 years. I place a good deal of importance on MacDougall research as it is totally objective and is not influenced by the next investment banking deal. (MacDougall does no investment banking.) As well, I read what gurus (Jimmy Rogers, Don Coxe, Warren Buffet, Marc Faber etc …) are saying. After all this, I come up with my own strategies and recommendations, all the while keeping it simple and following a high quality, disciplined approach."

What makes a good or bad retail broker?
"A good retail broker is a highly ethical, financially wise individual who has experience in the psychology of the market place. He must have a discerning eye to be able to detect the impostor and he must be a private financial investigator. He is passionate about his job and enjoys the personal contact with clients. I've always been impressed by retail brokers who are chosen by other brokers retiring from the business to manage

their accounts. Upon scrutiny, these brokers, by and large, have integrity, humility, patience, intelligence, experience, intuition and discipline. Good brokers, whether it comes from experience or intuition, have a penchant for anticipating where and when a stock will move. There is always a reason – led by events and demands in the real world, on Main Street or Bay Street. The trick is to see it before it happens. Good brokers will do that. There are brokers who will find a beaten down stock at the bottom of the St. Lawrence and investigate the company to see if it merits following for a recovery. These situations can be hugely profitable if they make it ... but there is a greater degree of risk associated with this type of investment. Good brokers are always looking for these underwater cases... They are always looking...plain and simple."

Who enjoys or dislikes retail broking?
"You've got to be able to get along with all kinds of people, and know how to handle all sorts of situations. Perhaps this is one of the attractions of this type of work – things are always different, each day brings something new. It is demanding and stressful, but when approached with passion, it is rewarding and great fun.

You have to like the stock market – the action of it, the excitement of it, the intrigue and the efficiency of it. In the end, you're helping people achieve greater financial security through a disciplined approach to financial markets. What could be more rewarding and enjoyable than helping people in this way? By and large, the people in the brokerage industry are hard-working, well educated, community minded, knowledgeable and ethical people who are in the business to help others attain financial success while achieving some financial success themselves. I have been fortunate in that my family has been in the business for years, from my grandfathers, father, uncle, cousin and brother… so it's in my blood and, if you grow up with this background, there's a certain genetic interest and passion for the business."

Timothy E. Price

Education:
BComm (Honours), Queen's University (1979)
CA, Institute of Chartered Accountants of Ontario (1983)
FCSI, Canadian Securities Institute (1988)
CFA designation, AIMR (1992)

Experience:
Investment Research, Rowe & Pitman – London, England (1980)
Staff Accountant, Coopers & Lybrand – Toronto (1980-82)
Audit Senior, Cooper & Lines – Bermuda (1982-84)
Controller, MacDougall, MacDougall & MacTier Inc. – Montreal (1984-90)
Investment Advisor and Portfolio Manager, MacDougall, MacDougall & MacTier Inc. – Montreal 1990-)

Current job:
President & Chief Executive Officer, MacDougall, MacDougall & MacTier Inc. – Montreal (2002-)

How would you describe the function of a retail broker in the financial world? Why does this profession and set of responsibilities exist in this way?

"The basic job of a retail broker is to give financial advice to clients. This advice can include suggestions about just about anything 'financial' (e.g. life insurance, real estate, borrowing strategies, budgeting), but there is a focus on *investment* advice, i.e. the selection of marketable securities to form a portfolio. As the four institutional 'pillars' of the Canadian financial industry (i.e. investment dealers, life insurance companies, banks and trust companies) have merged and as the number of retail financial products has proliferated, the distinctions between the various financial service providers has become blurred. For these reasons, a Canadian 'broker' can be found selling all kinds of financial products, from mutual funds, to insurance, to his own advisory services (or a mix). In some business models, the broker's role is to gather assets, not manage them. Nevertheless, the more traditional approach is still practised at many firms, whether as fee based portfolio management or as commission-based trading. At our firm and in my own business, there is a mix of these approaches, with 'retail broking' usually being identified by per trade compensation to the broker. This transaction-based approach can work best for certain clients. For instance, they may want to be more connected to each investment decision, or they may be the best judge of their own risk tolerance, or they may be a sophisticated investor who can add (specific or general) value to the decision-making process. For some clients with a long term approach and low trading volumes, choosing the per trade approach may be cost efficient. From the advisor's point of view, some brokers *only* fit into the retail broking category because of their specialization. For example, some brokers are explicitly *not* portfolio managers and have chosen to specialize in certain kinds of stocks: e.g. junior mining companies. It would not make sense to call them, or pay them as, investment counsellors."

How would you describe the job of a retail broker from a mechanical and day-to-day perspective?

"There are a number of aspects to the job. Keeping up to date with financial markets (including commodity and fixed income markets) and with individual companies is critical. A part of that task is to look constantly for new investment opportunities. The broker's in-house research department is an obvious starting point, but there are other sources of information – including specialty newsletters, personal contacts in specific industries and company presentations. Brokers need to filter all of this information to benefit their clients. In providing service to the client, there are a number of tasks, including keeping clients informed about opportunities, making sure their administrative concerns are met, and re-assessing their needs and risk profile. In addition, there is the constant search for new clients."

What makes a good or bad retail broker?

"A good broker is responsive and proactive. Clients want their brokers to be available for calls and questions – and they want to be called about new developments. They also want their more routine, but nevertheless important needs met: e.g. performance reporting, tax reporting, trade clearing, cheque preparation etc ... There is also an analytical aspect to being a good broker. You have to be able to understand and analyze opportunities. You must have a feel for financial markets. Good brokers grow their book of clients over time, but their financial sophistication grows with experience."

Who enjoys or dislikes retail broking?

"Compared to a closely related field, investment counselling, retail broking is more sales-oriented. You are on the phone with clients selling ideas and yourself every day. For this reason, more extroverted, outgoing people are going to like it more. You are also more of a generalist and need to know a little about a lot: stocks, bonds, mutual funds and commodities. You should also be financially savvy. A good retail broker is usually clever with his own money as well as with his clients'. Compared to other financial careers, it is more entrepreneurial, risky and cyclical. You are not paid a salary the way many professionals are. While there is accountability and profit participation in other professions, retail broking is 'eat what you kill' in a more immediate way. For this reason, people who are personally cash flow sensitive should avoid it. In the same vein, worriers should probably not choose this profession. Stocks go up and down. If this is going to keep you awake at night, this is not the profession for you."

Job Ideas

Key resource
Investment Dealers' Association of Canada www.ida.ca

Groups
BMO Nesbitt Burns www.nesbittburns.com
Caldwell Securities et al. (Toronto and branches across Ontario) www.caldwellsecurities.com
CIBC Wood Gundy www.woodgundy.com
Desjardins www.desjardins.com
Edward Jones (branches across Canada) www.edwardjones.com
First Associates/Rockwater (Toronto, Montreal, Calgary, Vancouver and branches across Canada) www.firstassociates.com
Golden Capital Securities (Vancouver) www.goldencapital.com
Hampton Securities (Toronto, Montreal) www.hamptonsecurities.com
Haywood Securities (Vancouver, Calgary and Toronto) www.haywood.com
Jones, Gable and Company (Toronto, Vancouver, Montreal and branches across Ontario) www.jonesgable.com
Laurentian www.vmbl.ca
MacDougall, MacDougall & MacTier Inc. (Toronto; Montreal; London, ON and Quebec City) www.3macs.com
National Bank Financial www.nbfinancial.com/
Northern Securities (Toronto, Vancouver and Calgary) www.northernsi.com
Odlum Brown (Vancouver & branches across BC) www.odlumbrown.com
Peters & Co. (Calgary) www.petersco.com
RBC Dominion Securities www.rbcinvestments.com
Research Capital (Toronto, Montreal, Calgary and Vancouver plus branches across Ontario) www.researchcapital.com
Scotia McLeod www.scotiamcleod.com

5. Money Management

Money management is the business of managing money for clients (i.e. buying and selling financial instruments for them on a discretionary basis). A 'client' can be a high net worth individual or an institutional client like a pension fund or mutual fund company. There are a lot of different terms synonymous to 'money manager', including 'portfolio manager', 'investment manager' and 'investment counsellor'. There is also a real spectrum of actual jobs within this field.

A money manager with individual clients (let's call him a 'Tier 1' money manager – this term is mine) may be little different than a retail broker. He will buy and sell stocks (and other instruments) for clients who are people. Generally, an individual must have a minimum liquid net worth ($200,000+) to hire a money manager. Given the degree of service and the level of customization involved, it would not be possible for an individual money manager to have an infinite number of clients. A 'pure' money manager will not have an in-house ability to execute trades, but will employ third party brokers to do so. Some individuals inside retail broking firms act as money managers (*de facto* or explicitly), but regulators frown upon this practice because of the conflict of interest between trade-oriented, per trade-compensated brokers and discretion-possessing managers.

Next, there are Tier 2 money managers who work for institutional clients and tend not to deal with individuals. They may work directly for an institutional client (e.g. a portfolio manager at the Caisse who manages a part of the Caisse's money), or they may work indirectly for a client (e.g. a portfolio manager at an independent firm like Jarislowsky Fraser that manages all sorts of pension fund assets on an arm's length basis). Even a mutual fund company may outsource the management of some of its funds to third parties and focus its efforts on marketing those funds to clients. Many clients will be large enough to justify their own money management staff if they so wish and, as a result, will always have the option of bringing the money management function in-house, or outsource it to third parties, or develop a hybrid of these two approaches. (Even when everything is outsourced, clients will often maintain a skeleton crew in order to monitor the performance of the third party managers.) Tier 2 managers will buy and sell stocks discretionarily for their institutional clients in much the same way as a Tier 1 manager would. The level of sophistication of both money manager and client increases as one passes from Tier 1 to Tier 2. (Please note: 'sophistication' does not mean skill, intelligence or results. It only means that possible investment strategies are more diverse and that the reporting/evaluation will be more detailed and technical. Even a large individual account will not have as many options in terms of diversification, derivative overlay strategies, etc … as a fund, nor will an individual demand the same kind of reporting or performance review as, say, a pension fund.) There are also other Tier 2 money managers who specialize in non-equity asset classes, e.g. fixed income. They rarely have individual clients.

Over and above these Tier 2 specialists, there are Tier 3 money managers who oversee very large funds' allocations between various Tier 2 managers (in-house managers, third party mangers or a mix of both). In addition to choosing *personnel*, they choose the allocation of assets between various *asset class* contenders for those dollars: e.g. various Tier 2 specialities (equity, fixed income etc ...) and other asset classes not usually included in the term 'money management' (e.g. real estate investing; what is called 'private equity' in this book). Tier 3 is money management in the broadest sense of the term and every option is on the table: public equity, private equity, fixed income (liquid and illiquid), real estate – all of which can be done in-house by the fund in question or farmed out to third parties. In Canada, think Caisse, Teachers, Canada Pension Plan and OMERS.

Like retail brokers, the money manager should know all aspects of his client's financial picture and invest according to the client's financial situation, anticipated liabilities and goals or, in the case of a mutual fund client, market positioning. The goals and the review process is much more elaborate than for retail broking. The investment criteria can be a mixture of performance objectives, risk tolerance, prohibitions (e.g. regarding investment concentration or certain kinds of stocks) and reporting methods.

There is more prestige to money management than retail broking. Retail broking still has a bit of a 'bucket shop' stigma. Before the days of external regulation and internal firm compliance, retail brokers were notorious for churning accounts (i.e. buying and selling client's holdings in order to generate per trade revenue), selling inappropriate investments to vulnerable or unsophisticated clients or even worse offences (e.g. front running – buying stock before a client does in order to squeeze out a tiny profit). Needless to say, this sort of thing still goes on, but much, much less than before. Even though some of the past abuses were perpetrated by retail brokers *acting as money managers* (how else would they have the discretionary ability to make trades?), money management as a profession is generally unstigmatized by these practices.

Money managers will also tend to have more education than retail brokers. Retail brokers need only have passed two courses (see above) to practise their profession – and many have done just that, while money managers will tend to have a post-graduate degree and/or the CFA. When working within a traditional brokerage, money managers are required to have experience and additional post-Canadian Securities Course education (i.e. the CFA or some combination of Canadian industry courses like the Investment Management Techniques Course and the Portfolio Management Techniques Course). There is a lot of pressure to obtain the CFA. When working for a 'pure' money management firm, the requirements are less strict, but are nevertheless more demanding than for retail broking. The atmosphere of an investment management firm is also more formal than a retail broking firm. Some people will like the formality and the academic environment; others won't.

(The discussion below looks at investment management as though one manager were trusted with the entirety of a client's wealth, i.e. in the role of a 'Tier 3' manager. As previously stated, different 'Tier 2' managers will often specialize in one asset class – e.g. in equity or fixed income – and the client will do the 'Tier 3' manager's job of asset allocation by assigning certain amounts to each specialized manager.)

Investment management has been greatly affected by the development of portfolio theory and formalization of procedure in the 1950's, 1960's and 1970's.

Investment managers make an even bigger deal out of 'know the client' than retail brokers. Ideally, each portfolio under management should have a formal, lengthy investment policy statement.

After assessing the client's situation, the next step in building a portfolio is to decide upon the portfolio's asset allocation between fixed income instruments, equity and 'other' (real estate, income trusts, private equity, derivatives). Ideally, this should be done in a scientific way. Studies have found that a large part of a portfolio's return comes from asset allocation decisions. Historical or prospective data about the returns and risks of asset classes (usually measured by standard deviation) can be combined to present a graphical picture of all possible portfolio mixes. The most desirable ones dominate others by having more return for the same risk, or the same return for less risk. The client's return expectations can be plotted on the same basis as a function of what amount of increased return he will require for a given amount of additional risk. When the line of optimal portfolios intersects with the client's indifference curve, bingo! that portfolio has the right characteristics for that client. (I have to believe that this is often done in a much more shorthand fashion, but this is the principle that underlies the process.)

Once asset allocation is 'done' (it will always be revisited), the money manager has to choose individual assets within the asset class. The style in which this selection is done will vary greatly by manager. For equity, it can be divided thus:
- Passive
- Active
  - Value
  - Growth

- Mixes of all of the above

A passive style tries to track or mimic the returns of a large index as closely as possible. Management fees are generally much lower than for actively managed accounts. An active style manager tries to find individual investments that for one reason or other will offer attractive returns. Managers that look for companies that are growing at rates not reflected in their stock prices are growth-oriented. Managers that look for companies where the underlying business is more valuable than the market is currently acknowledging are value-oriented.

On one side, the day-to-day life of an investment manager is focussed on the market and opportunities to buy or sell securities and, on the other, on client relations. Good performance without salesmanship will be unrewarding for the manager and weak performance can be mitigated by good PR.

Culture

I've found money management to be the most formal of the financial professions. This formality can manifest itself as quiet confidence, pride and bookishness. (On the subject of bookishness, I once talked to a money manager who was reading *Paris 1919: Six Months That Changed the World* by Richard Holbrooke. Meeting someone who was reading an academic book like that was unique in my time in finance.) In the bad cases, however, it becomes stiffness and self-importance. A few practitioners that I've met have been the "I know better and let me tell you how" type. These guys are used to managing millions of dollars and making yea or nay decisions on whether to fund all sorts of projects: new equity deals, new debt deals, private equity funds in the process of being organized. They also work everyday with brokers and traders and have a lot of bargaining power with them. It can't help but have an effect. For a money manager, the key is results and they usually keep track of these carefully and scientifically. If you can stay in business over long periods and have the results to show why, you're going to have a great reputation as a money manager.

Scott Fraser

Education:
BComm, McGill University (1951)

Experience:
Co-founder and investment counsellor, Jarislowsky Fraser (1958-1978)
Investment counsellor, A. Scott Fraser Investment Management (& other firms) (1978-2003)

Current job:
Managing Director, MacDougall Investment Counsel (2003-) & President, IFL Investment Foundation (Canada) Ltd.

How would you describe the function of a money manager in the financial world? Why does this profession and set of responsibilities exist in this way?

"The main product of a money manager is comfort. I don't calculate returns down to the last decimal place – although I'm proud of what I've been able to do. Within reason (of course), that's not what the profession is about. I have had clients who narrowly escaped the Holocaust in Europe and were very conservative with their money as a result. They wanted that extra security. As they got older, I told them – as I tell my other clients – to spend. One's ability to enjoy money through consumption declines with age and it is a shame to scrimp and save right to the end for no useful purpose. Being that sounding board for comfort and advice about the use and deployment of money is what money management is all about."

How would you describe the job of a money manager from a mechanical and day-to-day perspective?

"I have been in this business for decades so a given minute or hour of my time is not ultra-valuable. I know my clients; they know me and what I've done for them. As a result, I don't bother them with phone calls and meetings. On the investment front, I have had a lot of time to figure out what kind of companies I like and which ones I don't. In my view, there are three kinds of companies: those that are doing *what they should*, those that *aren't doing what they should* and those that *are doing what they should not be doing*. I avoid the third group categorically, and I don't feel I add a lot of value to the first. With the second group, I try to act as a catalyst investor. I try to re-focus management on positive free cash flow and returning that money to investors when it cannot be properly deployed within the company. (Editor's note: For a chart that Scott Fraser uses to analyze company performance, see end of profile.) Identifying these companies takes time, but that time is spent intensively over a short period. It is not a day-to-day activity. Similarly, talking to management about what they should be doing is not massively time consuming, nor is it a daily activity. But it is a big part of what I do."

What makes a good or bad money manager?
"Apart from the stuff that everyone should do with public information, a good money manager takes the time to get to know company management *personally*. There are certain sectors that I invest in where I have taken the time to get to know management and find out what is bugging them, where their problems are. This contact makes all the difference when it comes to investing in a sector. Of course, one can be wrong about people's character from time to time, but that

doesn't invalidate the approach. I also try to use a personal approach to changing a company's policies, although once or twice (in really unacceptable situations) I have threatened litigation or a public fight. You can't shrink from those cases either. A bad money manager lets a bad situation fester or explains it away by attributing it to impersonal 'market forces'. There is one such situation that I know of where action by a large shareholder should have been taken and it wasn't. His clients were badly served, as were the other shareholders of the company in question. Of course, not understanding that there is a problem in the first place is an even worse mistake."

Who enjoys or dislikes money management?
"Money management is a great field if you succeed in it. If you do well, everyone loves you. You can be difficult, dogmatic or even an appalling person, and you can get away with it. For this reason, I think it is a great field for individualists. You have a chance to go against the crowd and if you succeed, you've made a living on your own terms and helped your clients achieve their objectives. Not bad for a day's work."

Money management in a sentence:
"The business of money management is providing comfort to your clients."

Addendum:
Director's Cash Flow Statement

<u>Sources of Cash</u>

<u>From Operations</u>   <u>Capital Items</u>

Net Profit + Depreciation   New Equity + New Debt

<u>Applications of Cash</u>

− (Fixed Asset Addition (Net)) + Equity/Debt Retirement + Dividends)

= +/− Working Capital

Note: Increases in excessive working capital provide no economic benefit

[Editor's note: Mr. Fraser literally has this chart on his office wall.]

Patrick Bernes

Education:
BComm degree (Finance Major), Concordia University (2000)
CFA designation, AIMR (2003)

Experience:
Compliance Analyst – TAL Global Asset Management, Mtl (2002-2003)
Senior Analyst, Office of the Chief Investment Officer – TAL Global Asset Management, Montreal (2004-)

Current job:
Senior Analyst, Office of the Chief Investment Officer – TAL Global Asset Management, Montreal (2004-)

How would you describe the function of a money manager in the financial world? Why does this profession and set of responsibilities exist in this way?

"Money managers are tasked with managing large sums of institutional funds, and typically specialize in one particular asset class. In larger shops, the money managers are largely freed up of marketing and sales functions and left to focus specifically on managing the assets assigned to them. This profession exists thanks to the widely held beliefs that actively managed assets yield superior returns over time; that talent yields results and asset management is best left to the professionals."

How would you describe the job of a money manager from a mechanical and day-to-day perspective?

"Money managers must be 'in tune' with what happens in the capital markets. By deciphering signals from a web of contacts and information sources, managers must ultimately forecast asset prices and implement trade ideas within their portfolios. Valuation models are used to generate and validate decisions. A typical equity manager manages a portfolio based on a model portfolio and passes on trade execution and (account) allocation responsibilities to middle office and trading resources."

What makes a good or bad money manager?

"Good managers are decisive by nature. They can articulate clearly and defend their investment ideas, and do not get overly discouraged in bad times, recognizing that 'bad times' come with the territory. Bad managers cannot explain in 'plain language' their investment process. They act impulsively, and take on additional risk in order to make up for poor performance."

Who enjoys or dislikes money management?

"People who enjoy money management share a passion for investing and a general appreciation of problem solving. It is more of an art form than a science. People from diverse backgrounds end up in this realm. People with fragile egos that do not like being thrust into the spotlight or assume career risks are not cut out for this type of work."

Money management in a sentence:

"Money management is the introverted cousin of the 'sell side', where time is measured in months, not minutes; and success is the result of disciplined analysis; never the closing of the 'deal'."

Job Ideas

Charting the world of money management from a job search or market study perspective is very tricky because the pension and mutual funds that control a given amount of money can keep all decision-making functions in-house, or outsource much or all decision-making to third parties – who in turn can outsource again. (Terms like 'assets under management' are also tricky to evaluate, for this reason and due to the tendency of firms to include co-managed funds etc ... in this figure.) Finding out the 'brand name' of a given pool of money is often just the beginning: it may take quite a bit of digging to find where the asset allocation is actually done and where the individual securities of an asset class are in fact selected and monitored.

There are also bank-owned firms (many that used to be independent) that manage bank-branded mutual funds, as well as third party funds and individual accounts. It is not clear to the outsider how these groups interact with the rest of their parent bank or with the rest of its wealth management units (e.g. retail brokers, specialized private banking units etc ...).

On top of this web of relationships, there are money managers who focus on direct relationships with high net worth individuals and who may not have any retail 'face' visible to the public.

Remember that (capital) barriers to entry are quite low for this business and many firms will be quite small. This makes for many possible employers, but their personnel needs are unfortunately also small.

Of these hundred of firms, these are only some of the larger and more prominent ones.

Key resources
Investment Counsel Association of Canada
  www.investmentcounsel.org
Financial Services Canada 2004/2005 – Canada's Definitive Financial Services Industry Reference Directory (7th edition). Micromedia ProQuest, 2004.

Bank-Owned/Associated Firms
Jones Heward/Bank of Montreal (Toronto, Calgary) www.jonesheward.com
Natcan/National Bank (Montreal) www.natcan.com
RBC Asset Management Inc /Royal Bank www.rbcam.com
Scotia Cassels/Bank of Nova Scotia (Toronto) www.scotiacassels.com
TAL/CIBC (Toronto and Montreal) www.tal.ca
TD Asset Management www.tdassetmanagement.com

Pension Funds
BIMCOR – Bell's pension fund (Montreal) 514.394.4750
Caisse/Caisse de dépôt et placement du Québec (Montreal, Quebec City) www.lacaisse.com
CN (Montreal) 1.800.361.0739
CPP (Canada Pension Plan) Investment Board (Toronto) www.cppib.ca
Hospitals of Ontario Pension Plan (HOOPP) (Toronto) www.hoopp.com
OMERS/Ontario Municipal Employees Retirement System (Toronto) www.omers.com
Public Sector Pensions Investment Board (Montreal) www.investpsp.com
Teachers/Ontario Teachers' Pension Plan (Toronto) www.otpp.com

Advisors and Mutual Funds
AGF Management Limited (Toronto) www.agf.com
Beutel, Goodman & Company Ltd. (Toronto) www.beutel-can.com

Bluewater (Toronto) 416.599.5300
Burgundy (Toronto and Montreal) www.burgundy-asset.com
CI Mutual Funds Inc. (Toronto) www.cifunds.com
Co-operators Investment Counselling Limited (Guelph) www.cooperatorsinvestment.ca
Cundill Investment Research Ltd. (Vancouver) www.cundill.com
Dundee Wealth Management (Toronto) www.dundeewealth.com
Goodman and Company Investment Counsel see Dundee Wealth Management
Gluskin Sheff + Associates Inc. (Toronto) www.gluskinsheff.com
Greystone Capital Management Inc. (Regina) 306.779.6400
Gryphon (Toronto, Montreal and Halifax) www.gryphon.ca
HSBC Asset Management (Toronto, Montreal, Vancouver, Calgary) www.hsbc.ca
Howson Tattersall (Toronto) www.htic.ca
Jarislowsky Fraser (Toronto, Montreal and Calgary) www.jfl.ca
McLean Budden (Toronto, Montreal and Vancouver) www.mcleanbudden.com
Montrusco Bolton (Montreal, Quebec, Toronto, Calgary, Halifax, Moncton) www.montruscobolton.com
Phillips, Hager & North (Toronto, Montreal, Vancouver, Calgary, Victoria) www.phn.com
Pictet (Montreal) 514.288.8161
UBS (Toronto, Montreal) www.ubs.co

Section IV. Private Equity

In this book, I have used the term 'private equity' to apply to three activities (venture capital, merchant banking and mezzanine). See Terminology, p. 16.

Unlike a holistic operating company or a bank, there is usually a fairly strict legal division between a private equity group and 'its' money. In order to begin business, a private equity group will raise a fund composed of money from pension funds and other groups. (In the past, some private equity groups have been funded through public companies – e.g. Clairvest, Benvest – or 'evergreen' funds – e.g. NovaCap, but this arrangement is relatively rare and becoming rarer.) High net worth individuals are another source of funds for private equity players. While this money will usually be a small portion of a fund's total commitment, it can have a very important networking function. If an executive or entrepreneur has put money into a fund, he will be very keen to see that fund succeed. As a result, the private equity group gains access to the investor's network of business contacts and associates. When a question, problem or opportunity comes up that is relevant to that network, the private equity group will have an edge that no amount of money can buy.

Each investor in a private equity fund makes a dollar commitment to the fund that is generally not disbursed and remains contingent until each actual investment for the fund is found. The idea is to invest the money in private companies, help the companies increase in value (especially in the case of venture capitalists and merchant bankers), realize on the investment (through the sale of the whole company, its recapitalization, a sale of the discrete instrument used by the private equity firm or a buyback of the instrument in question by the company) and return the (hopefully large amount of) money to the fund's investors.

The private equity firm makes money by charging a management fee to investors on the amount of money committed (or actually disbursed, or a blend of these approaches), by management fees charged to the portfolio companies (perennially and/or for each intervention in the company's affairs by the private equity professionals) and, most importantly, by receiving a 'carry' (or 'carried interest') at the expense of the investors' return. The carry is earned when the investors in fact attain a certain hurdle rate of return. All of the money earned to return the investors' principal and reach the hurdle is given back to the investors. After that point, the private equity firm receives a pre-determined percentage of the money generated from the sale of the fund's investments, and the investors receive the balance. Due to the fact that each fund raised has a fixed dollar commitment, fixed investment period (during which the investors' commitments must be spent or lost) and fixed life (by the end of which the money must be returned to the investors), private equity groups tend to live fund to fund. If a group is not 're-funded' after their last fund is invested and sold, they are out of business.

Culture

The number of private equity professionals is much less than the number of investment bankers, corporate bankers, equity analysts, retail brokers or money managers. Private equity firms are usually partnerships of relatively few people – especially in Canada – so what those particular partners say, goes. Also, very few people start out in private equity. Many are ex-investment or corporate bankers. As a result, they arrive at their private equity job with a 'built-in' culture. In addition, of all financial professions, private equity probably attracts the greatest number of non-financial people to its ranks. An 'operator' is most welcome inside a merchant bank. The financial types value his expertise in production (or retail or distribution), union negotiation, supplier relations, marketing – all sorts of tangible operating experience. The same is true with a more technological spin in the world of venture capital. The net result of these facts is a less stereotype-able culture and more idiosyncratic profession – but that doesn't mean that individual firms won't have strong identities.

6. Venture Capital

Venture capitalists invest in the equity of start-up and early stage companies in order to resell them in a given time frame. As explained above, most VC's raise money from institutional investors and wealthy private individuals. Some large (tech) corporations have a VC arm in-house. The goal of these divisions is less financial (i.e. earn IRR on a fund and move on) and more strategic ("What technology is out there and what should the parent company be doing with/about it?").

Venture capitalists tend to be quite specialized. There are two ways that the population of groups in the industry can be divided: by stage of targeted investment and by industry specialization. The commonly used investment stages are seed, start-up, early and late. 'Seed' money is funding needed to found a company (incorporation, initial office expenses, business plan creation) and is often quite modest. Non-institutional 'angel' investors (often retired entrepreneurs and executives) are much more active in this field than professional or institutional groups. The 'angels' often offer informal business, strategic and financing advice to the founding entrepreneurs. 'Start-up' investing furnishes the money needed for R&D/prototypes, pre-marketing and related activities (more business plans, more marketing plans, feasibility studies, travel etc …). 'Early' investing furnishes the money for commercialization and 'late' stage investing is often semi-optional bridge financing before a company is taken public or sold to a strategic player. A firm that specializes in one stage may not invest in the other stages at all. The instruments (and so the venture capitalists' specialities) can vary by stage. It also makes sense to put similar risk/return investments together in one portfolio. Having one 'hail Mary' start-up investment in a portfolio of late-stage investments is an invitation to lose money and not have it recoupable by the less risky, less rewarding late stage investments. Being in the start-up business and having 20 such investments, on the other hand, makes it likely that the large winners will more than compensate for the total losers.

Venture capital firms can also be divided by industry focus. Given the technical nature of this type of investing, some firms will not invest outside of their area of expertise. Venture capitalists often invest in technologies that are unproven technologically or unproven in the market (or both). Who knows if Gizmo X will indeed be adopted by the telecom/PC/software industry? No one – but a former operator or technical person from that field has the best chance of assessing it. These professionals can also tap into their network of still-in-industry professionals for invaluable insight. Venture capital firms rely more on these in-house technical professionals more than many other investment fields (e.g. merchant banking, mezzanine, lending, public company investing).

Given the early stage of these investments (the companies in question are almost always pre-profit and frequently pre-revenue), the venture capitalists' money almost always goes into the portfolio company's coffers via an issue of shares from treasury. Although venture capitalists are always looking for equity – i.e. theoretically infinite – returns, they may use convertible debt as a structuring tool. By investing in a company through a convertible debt instrument, they get the best of both worlds. If the company does well, they will convert their debt into equity and participate in the upside as equity owners. If the company does badly, their 'new money' convertible instrument will rank ahead of the initial shareholders' pure equity.

The Canadian venture capital market has one peculiarity: many of the VC funds are 'labour sponsored'. Labour sponsored funds offer investors an immediate tax credit and market this feature to retail investors.

Venture capitalists experience a wide variance of return from -100% to many times their investment. As a general rule of thumb, of ten investments, 6-8 will be total failures. The key is to get some money from the others – and have one, two or three real winners. Venture capitalists will take minority positions in companies (but will usually have board representation), often invest alongside others and have 15-30 companies per fund.

For culture, see the introduction to Section IV. Private Equity.

Andrew Waitman

Education:
Bachelor of Applied Science (Electrical Engineering), University of Waterloo (1987)
MBA (with distinction), Richard Ivey School of Business (University of Western Ontario) (1992)
CFA designation, AIMR (1998)

Experience:
Nortel Networks, Designed and developed telephony software – Ottawa (1985-1990)
Senior Associate (Derivatives Group), Citibank Canada – Toronto (1992-1994)
Senior Equity Analyst (Technology), Eagle & Partners – Toronto (1994-1996)

Current job:
Managing Partner, Celtic House Venture Partners – Ottawa (1996-)

How would you describe the function of a venture capitalist in the financial world? Why does this profession and set of responsibilities exist in this way?

"The venture capitalist is part banker (exercising investment judgement), part engineer (identifying what to build), part management consultant (providing strategic and tactical advice), part businessman (extending a business network of valuable contacts) and part coach (encouraging, facilitating and driving to success). To build high technology companies from scratch in a dynamic and complex business ecosystem takes a myriad of skills, judgement and entrepreneurial passion. Because the stakes are enormous and the challenges extreme, the appropriate skill sets are rare. The business is about predictions, which are particularly difficult to make."

How would you describe the job of a venture capitalist from a mechanical and day-to-day perspective?

"The venture capitalist spends a great deal of time engaging and communicating with people in discussion of ideas, opportunities and plans, which lead to a myriad of decisions. Decisions are the venture capitalists' most potent outcome. Decisions to invest, decisions to divest, decisions to hire, decisions to fire. In order to make valuable, helpful and constructive decisions, the venture capitalist must have the relevant information, contextual understanding and measured judgement. These are gained by listening to management both inside and outside the boardroom, participating in industry events and keeping abreast of the competitive landscape."

What makes a good or bad venture capitalist?

"A good venture capitalist is someone who facilitates the creation of a company with a set of constituents and parameters that allow for all parties to win. A good venture capitalist appreciates the inexactness of the art of venture capital while providing the discipline of good investment practices. A dangerous venture capitalist is one who does not know what he does not know."

Who enjoys or dislikes being a venture capitalist?

"A venture capitalist is a generalist, facilitating investor. A hands-on executive who has a high need to control would not enjoy the business of venture capital."

Venture capital in a sentence:

"Venture capital is a key constituent of a robust modern economy."

Mila M. Felcarek

Education:
Master in Management and Engineering, Czech Technical University – Prague (1987)
MBA, Middlesex University – London (1992)

Experience:
Assistant Lecturer, Czech Technical University – Prague (1988-90)
Finance Manager, Imperial Chemical Industry (ICI) – Prague (1992-94)
Director of Finance, European Privatization and Investment Corporation (EPIC) – Prague (1994-1996)
Investment Manager, Bell Canada International – Montreal (1997-2000)
Director (Private Equity & Venture Capital Secondary Investing), CDP Capital – Montreal (2001-2004)

Current job:
Managing Director, Trammell-Shott Capital Management – Montreal (2004-)

How would you describe the function of a venture capitalist in the financial world? Why does this profession and set of responsibilities exist in this way?

"Venture capitalists (VCs) are specialty investors who specialise in investing in young, fast growing companies that have the potential for substantial growth, a dominant market position and ultimately an initial public offering (IPO) or a trade sale. These investors are in the business of allocating scarce capital to the 'tadpoles' of the commercial world. VCs are only interested in businesses that can grow significantly! If you're a corner grocery store, sushi bar or lemonade stand, seek your financing elsewhere (unless you plan to become a chain of 500 outlets). The venture capitalist's primary motive is to make a significant return on their investment (frankly, none of the 'betterment of society' lipstick story really applies)."

How would you describe the job of a venture capitalist from a mechanical and day-to-day perspective?

"The venture capitalist, in addition to supplying the company with money, also assists in its business: planning and bringing industry knowledge to the table (as well as experience in growing businesses). The younger the company, the more of an operational involvement on the part of the VC will be required. The VC will not only provide the capital a business requires, it will become a partner for life of the company. It will offer a valuable sounding board for ideas, insight on the direction of the marketplace, assistance with developing business opportunities, business introductions, help with recruiting a world class management team. Finally, the VC will be able to offer help obtaining future rounds of financing and ultimately in achieving the point when the years of hard work are transformed into real value for the founders and managers of a business – the trade sale or IPO."

What makes a good or bad venture capitalist?

"Good or rather great VCs are those who have great returns on a consistent basis. From 1980 to 2001, the bottom quartile of VCs generated about a 3% return while top quartile ones produced annual rates of return of 23%. Those who are successful in the business of funding young companies typically understand the technological needs of society and in addition are gifted in art of building companies."

Who enjoys or dislikes being a venture capitalist?

"The potential risks of venture capital investing are great, thus VC professionals need to be highly selective when deciding which opportunities to pursue. VCs need to sift through hundreds of business opportunities presented to them each year. As a result of this it is essential for anyone intending to become a VC that they are of a patient breed, technology-savvy, disciplined and can make decisions without losing sleep over it."

Venture capital in brief:

"A venture capitalist is a fellow who signs the cheque for an exact sum of money, hands it over to an entrepreneur and in return takes an ownership position in a company of unknown value. In a sense, he is a financial artist performing a crazy form of dealmaking: buying dreams."

Job Ideas
Remember that many technology corporations have a VC unit in-house.

Key resource
Canada's Venture Capital & Private Equity Association
   www.cvca.ca

Groups
BDC – Venture Capital (Montreal, offices throughout
   Canada) www.bdc.ca
Celtic House (Toronto, Ottawa) www.celtic-house.com
Edgestone (Toronto, Montreal) www.edgestone.com
Fonds de solidarité FTQ (Montreal) www.fondsftq.com
GrowthWorks Capital (Toronto, Vancouver, Halifax,
   Saskatoon) www.growthworks.ca
GTI Capital (Montreal) www.gticapital.com
McLean Watson Capital (Toronto, Ottawa)
   www.mcleanwatson.com
Novacap (Montreal) www.novacap.ca
Primaxis Technology Ventures (Toronto) www.primaxis.com
Skypoint Capital Corporation (Montreal, Ottawa)
   www.skypointcorp.com
Teachers' Private Capital (Toronto) www.otpp.com
Trellis Capital Corporation (Toronto) www.trelliscapital.com
Vengrowth (Toronto, Ottawa) www.vengrowth.com
Ventures West (Toronto, Montreal, Vancouver, Ottawa)
   www.ventureswest.com

7. Merchant Banking

Merchant banking (also called 'working in private equity', buyouts or leveraged buyouts/LBOs) is the business of buying and selling the equity of (usually profitable) private companies. (There are many sub-specialities within this field and some groups may invest in public companies as well. This is called 'PIPE' investing: Private Investment in Public Equity. In addition, even funds that are focussed on investing in equity may themselves insert mezzanine or subordinated debt into a portfolio company in order to be able to take some money out of it on a tax efficient basis.) As explained above, merchant banks raise money from institutional investors and wealthy individuals.

Although there is a spectrum among groups, merchant banking groups tend to invest in relatively few companies (8-12 per fund), purchase a large percentage (up to 100%) of a company's equity and be very active on the boards of their portfolio companies. This intense involvement of the professionals in their portfolio companies' affairs distinguishes merchant banking from almost all other types of investing (e.g. venture capital, mezzanine, equity investing in public companies, lending) and earns the activity its other name, 'buyouts'.

The term 'leveraged buyout' (or 'LBO') arises from the usual practice of making investments only in leveraged companies. (Leverage is usually inserted into a portfolio company by incorporating a Newco, funding it with the debt and equity dollars needed to buy the portfolio company, finalizing the sale as a company-to-company transaction and then merging the two companies. Any equity left in the hands of the selling shareholders is rolled on a tax-free basis into shares of Newco.) Leverage increases returns and, of course, risk. A lot of time can be spent structuring transactions so that the debt ends up in the right place (i.e. where it can be deducted from income to reduce income tax). Other goals often have to be met, too. For instance, if the firm is buying from an owner-operator, the merchant banking firm might not want to buy all of the equity from him and be left without an incentivized and knowledgeable manager. All sorts of instruments can be designed to keep the owner-operator involved over the short or long term. The simplest would be a simple roll of the owner-operator's existing equity into equity of the new, leveraged company. More complex instruments give the owner-operator incentives to meet certain short-term targets in order to get his full purchase price. This type of instrument is often called an 'earn-out' or 'conditional balance of sale'.

Even in Canada, there is quite a bit of specialization within the merchant banking field. Even an unequivocally 'good' deal (from a rate of return point of view) will not fit all firms. A firm's criteria depend on all sorts of things. Firstly, the merchant bank has presented itself in a certain way to its investors. This positioning will be determined by the expertise of the firm's merchant bankers, by their feeling of where the best returns are to be found, by their perception of what the market is looking for in terms of an investment in the merchant banking area and by the existing competition. Secondly, the size of a fund will limit a firm's scope. Generally a firm will only be allowed (or want) to invest a certain percentage of their fund in a single deal. Given this limitation and merchant banking's definition as taking large or control positions in equity, certain transactions will be too big for a given fund to acquire a large percentage of. On the other hand, if a company is too small (when measured in terms of dollars to be disbursed by the fund), the firm will have to decline. A fund does not want 20-30 tiny investments! Some funds are also prohibited by their investors from certain types of specialized investments, e.g. real estate, oil & gas, mining.

A major preoccupation of merchant bankers is deal flow. Merchant bankers have to look at hundreds of deals in order to find ones that indeed fit their criteria. Deal flow is generated through investment bankers, personal contacts, professional contacts (i.e. lawyers and accountants) and general exposure of the firm. In order to keep pricing down and fees low, merchant bankers prefer to see as many deals as possible that are unbrokered and exclusive, or 'proprietary'.

The day-to-day work of a merchant banker is composed of managing existing portfolio companies, sifting through new potential deals and closing actual (entrance and exit) transactions. On the portfolio side, the principal activities are attendance at board meetings and positioning the portfolio companies for sale. Merchant bankers try not to get involved too much in operations, although crises, intra-management disputes, poor performance and difficulty in recruiting managers may make greater involvement necessary. On the transaction side, valuation, structuring, negotiation, due diligence on target companies and securing the bank (and, if applicable, mezzanine) financing are the principal activities. Because merchant bankers will have to live with a very illiquid investment for many years, a lot of time is spent on 'due diligence'. (This 'due diligence' is much more intensive than investment bankers' due diligence.) Due diligence includes backward looking activities such as tax, accounting and environmental reviews and forward looking activities such as reviewing projections and the industry in question.

For culture, see the introduction to Section IV. Private Equity.

Louise Lalonde

Education:
BComm, HEC (University of Montreal)
CA, Ordre des comptables agréés du Québec (1985)

Experience:
Auditor, Samson Bélair – Montreal (1980-83)
Directeur, Quebec Securities Commission – Montreal (1983-87)
Directeur (Financial & Special Services), Samson Bélair/Deloitte & Touche – Montreal (1995-99)
Directeur Investissements, Fonds de solidarité FTQ – Montreal (1995-99)
CFO, Denharco – Montreal (1999-2000)

Current job:
Directeur, Investissements (Secteur manufacturier) – Capital d'Amérique/Caisse de Dépôt et Placement du Québec – Montreal (2000-)

How would you describe the function of a merchant banker in the financial world? Why does this profession and set of responsibilities exist in this way?

"In my opinion, my current job is not pure merchant banking. Although my organization invests in private companies, it does not take majority or control positions in them.[1] In my opinion, groups that aim to find and acquire control of companies are pure merchant banks. The creation of numerous buyout funds over the course of the last few years (in order to ex-

---

[1] Editor's note: Louise is unduly modest about the scope of her experience. Although she does not do buyouts, she directly invests in private companies like the buyout funds do and she has occasion to work on transactions with funds that do acquire control positions. She also supervises her fund's investment in other merchant banking and buyout funds – and so her views are especially valuable.

ploit a perceived opportunity in the private company space) has created a real demand for this kind of professional. The job consists of finding companies, analyzing them sufficiently to make a decision on whether to invest and at what price, negotiating the transaction, finding the third party financing (e.g. bank debt), following the company post-closing and sharing in the value creation."

How would you describe the job of a merchant banker from a mechanical and day-to-day perspective?

"I believe that a merchant bank must participate in its portfolio companies' value creation strategies *on a daily basis*. For example, if a company needs to improve its cost structure, the merchant bank must make sure that the mechanisms are in place to achieve this goal. If the company intends to pursue acquisitions, the merchant banker must participate in the search and negotiation of any transactions. If it is the top line that needs improving, the merchant banker must revisit the sales strategy and participate in the action plan."

What makes a good or bad merchant banker?

"A good merchant banker is someone who has worked in several fields in his or her career: e.g. consulting, finance, operations (inside a company), and who likes working with successful entrepreneurs. In my view, a good merchant banker is someone who could themselves be the CEO of a company or an entrepreneur and who has the ability to analyze all aspects of a business without being an expert in everything."

Who enjoys or dislikes being a merchant banker?

"Someone who likes routine and working on one single project at a time would not like merchant banking. Someone who wants to analyze everything in detail would not be a good merchant banker. And someone who is not ready to take risks *should not be* a merchant banker."

Charles Bougie

Education:
BComm, Concordia University (1995)
MBA, Richard Ivey School of Business (University of Western Ontario) (2001)

Experience:
Product coordinator and software trainer, Kabba Ilco – Montreal (1995-1997)
Customer service representative, Oakley – Montreal (1998)
Project Consultant, USC Consulting Group – Chicago (1998-1999)
Associate, Novacap – Montreal (2001-2004)

Current job:
Financial Services Manager (Equity Group), EDC – Ottawa (2004-)

How would you describe the function of a merchant banker in the financial world? Why does this profession and set of responsibilities exist in this way?

"The function of a merchant banker is to take investment risks that are beyond the threshold of an institutional investor. Merchant bankers usually invest in private companies that are more mature than ones that attract venture capital (e.g. profitable companies, turnarounds, management buyouts or 'other'). A merchant bank's cost of capital is usually higher than normal (e.g. public markets) and to mitigate the elevated risk, merchant bankers will usually get involved in management selection, as well as strategic and operational planning."

How would you describe the job of a merchant banker from a mechanical and day-to-day perspective?

"You can categorize day-to-day aspects of merchant banking in three distinctive steps. The first step is to look for opportunities for investment. Merchant bankers will see a lot of opportunities, but it is not easy to find ones that meet a particular fund's investment criteria. Once a good opportunity is found, the second step is to execute a transaction that appeals to both the investor and the investee. Once this is completed, merchant bankers will monitor the investment and will sometimes play an operational role in the investee company."

What makes a good or bad merchant banker?

"A good merchant banker is a well-rounded individual who has a good understanding of all the business issues that a company has to overcome to succeed. That said, merchant bankers usually work within a team and the most successful merchant banks consist of a small group of diverse individuals including generalists and specialists in finance, accounting, law, operations, marketing and other disciplines."

Who enjoys or dislikes being a merchant banker?

"A person who likes to deal with complex issues and who is very persistent and patient would like merchant banking. Individuals who like to see the fruit of their efforts immediately and do not like change will have a difficult time being merchant bankers as the investment cycle is on average seven to eight years, as opposed to an institutional investor who can buy and sell shares of a public company on the same day."

Merchant banking in a sentence:

Take 1: "Merchant banking is what Richard Gere did in the movie *Pretty Woman.*"

Take 2: "Merchant banking is investing capital while having the ability to direct an investee company towards areas that will bring it success over the course of 5-10 years."

Job Ideas

Key resource
Canada's Venture Capital & Private Equity Association
  www.cvca.ca

Groups
BMO Equity Partners (Toronto) www.nesbittburns.com
Borealis see OMERS
CAI (Toronto, Montreal, Vancouver) www.caifunds.com
Caisse/Caisse de dépôt et placement du Québec (Montreal,
  Quebec City)
CIBC Capital Partners (Toronto) www.cibcwm.com
Clairvest (Toronto) www.clairvest.com
Edgestone (Toronto, Montreal) www.edgestone.com
Novacap (Montreal) www.novacap.ca
OMERS/Ontario Municipal Employees Retirement System
  (Toronto) www.omers.com
Oncap (Toronto) www.oncap.com
ONEX (Toronto) www.onex.com
Scotia Merchant (Toronto) www.scotiamerchantcapital.com
TD Capital (Toronto) www.tdcapital.com
Teachers/Ontario Teachers' Pension Plan (Toronto)
  www.otpp.com
Torquest (Toronto) www.torquest.com
Triwest (Calgary) www.triwest.ca

8. Mezzanine

Mezzanine debt is an instrument that lies between pure equity and pure debt. Mezzanine funds invest via this type of debt, usually in private companies. The funds so invested can be used for many purposes. Often the mezzanine 'piece' is set up at the time of a company buyout by a merchant banking group and forms a part of the funds required to purchase the company. Like the senior debt, it will be 'forced down' into the target company (via the merger of a cash-capitalized Newco and the target operating company) and become a liability on its balance sheet. Mezzanine can be also be loaned to a firm that wants funds, has reached the limit of its senior debt borrowing power and doesn't want to (or can't) issue equity. As explained above, most mezzanine groups raise money from institutional investors and wealthy individuals, although some are run as divisions of traditional chartered banks and simply lend the banks' money.

Mezzanine lies between debt and equity in several ways. Firstly, the target return of a mezzanine provider is in between that of debt and equity. Currently, equity investors are looking for 25-35% from private companies and debt is quite cheap (usually less than 10%). Mezzanine holders look for returns in the 15-25% range. Secondly, the degree of control exercised by the mezzanine group on the investee company is also in between. Equity holders in private companies usually demand some board representation (and other rights); debt holders are usually limited to their contractual rights to get paid and to exercise certain specific remedies if they are not. From a control point of view, mezzanine holders are like debt holders when things go well and like equity holders as the picture worsens. (Their debt may even turn into equity in certain circumstances.) Thirdly, one of the mezzanine provider's principal instruments is 'equity-esque'. Usually the main investment is in debt with a high coupon (say, 12%). The remainder of the return is expected to come from warrants to purchase stock that are exerciseable under certain circumstances, e.g. the sale of the whole company. (One can see how mezzanine debt is oriented towards merchant banking and its purchase and sale of whole companies.) So, from a return point of view, when things go well, mezzanine players act more like equity players looking for upside and, when things go badly, more like debt players looking to get their capital back. For firms that aren't headed towards a full liquidity event, mezzanine firms can do 'money rental' deals (i.e. a higher coupon with no warrants). In this case, the provider's return is capped.

Like senior lenders, mezzanine players also impose covenants on their borrowers that must be met or they will be in breach.

For culture, see the introduction to Section IV. Private Equity.

John Bradlow

Education:
MBA, Harvard University (1970)
CA, Institute of Chartered Accountants of Ontario (1978)

Experience:
Hill Samuel – Johannesburg, South Africa (1972-1977)
Senior Vice-President (project finance, corporate finance, international division), Bank of Montreal – Toronto (1977-89)
President, First City Capital Markets – Toronto (1989-92)
Partner, Private Equity Management Corporation – Toronto (1992-98)
Partner, Private Equity Management Corporation/Penfund/CIBC – Toronto (1998-2000)

Current job:
Partner, Penfund Mezzanine Financing – Toronto (1998-)

How would you describe the function of a mezzanine lender in the financial world? Why does this profession and set of responsibilities exist in this way?

"The market for mezzanine capital exists because some private companies exhaust their senior debt capacity and are either unwilling or unable to raise equity, but still need capital. From a mezzanine investor's point of view, some of these companies offer good risk/return characteristics.

From an institutional point of view, mezzanine can be provided by traditional banks that hold the loan on their balance sheet (as BMO, CIBC, Roynat/Scotia and HSBC do) or by groups like ours that lend from a fund that will eventually be liquidated (including bank sponsored groups like TD Capital). Mezzanine lenders have been successful when they have been selective, entrepreneurial and personally involved in the upside and downside of their business. Successful lenders have also remained committed to the market and instrument, whereas some competitors have entered the market only to leave again."

How would you describe the job of a mezzanine lender from a mechanical and day-to-day perspective?
"The mezzanine lender has four main tasks: origination, negotiation with prospective clients, risk appraisal and due diligence, and documentation of deals. 'Origination' is just a fancy word for marketing. Negotiation involves agreeing on a term sheet (interest rate, extent of warrants, covenants etc ...). This term sheet is always subject to due diligence. Once a term sheet is agreed upon, we go to work appraising risk and completing full due diligence on the investee in question. Documentation is simply putting the final deal on paper with the help of lawyers. We do all these tasks daily."

What makes a good or bad mezzanine lender?
"Of the three main categories of private equity (venture capital, buyouts and mezzanine) only mezzanine has consistently provided acceptable returns to Canadian investors. Why is this? I see mezzanine as primarily a credit product; whereas the other two are primarily investment products or activities. This affects the kind of skills needed to succeed. For instance, in the venture capital world, sectoral knowledge is key and generic investment skills can be almost useless. In the mezzanine world, credit skills are key. In Canada, mezzanine has been able to achieve good results be-

cause there are a number of ex-commercial bankers who can and do work in mezzanine. In the other fields, the skills are rarer and the results suffer."

Who enjoys or dislikes mezzanine lending?

"The 'mezzanine mindset' is conservative and cautious. This is a game of singles and doubles. Our portfolio target is in the 18% range. If we suffer one write-off, the economics of the portfolio will be devastated. We simply can't afford to make a mistake. That is a tough proposition. The VCs and the buyout funds can take greater risk and suffer heavy losses on some investments because they can make them up with '10 baggers'. We can't. Someone who can work under these constraints will enjoy mezzanine lending."

Mezzanine in a sentence:

"For a private company that can't or doesn't want to raise private equity and that needs money, mezzanine is the only choice."

Richard Bradlow

Education:
BA, University of Western Ontario (1994)
MBA, Harvard University (1999)

Experience:
Co-Founder, Rivet Laundry (retailer of imported jeans & casual wear) – Montreal (1994-1997)
Associate Director (Investment Banking), Scotia Capital – Toronto (1999-2003)

Current job:
Principal, Penfund Mezzanine Financing – Toronto (2003)

How would you describe the function of a mezzanine lender in the financial world?

"A mezzanine lender provides capital to companies that have exhausted their ability to raise senior debt and do not want to or cannot raise equity."

Why does this profession and set of responsibilities exist in this way?

"There is a gap in the capital market spectrum between commercial bank debt and private equity. Mezzanine lenders target investments within this gap, with a commensurate risk and return profile."

How would you describe the job of a mezzanine lender from a mechanical and day-to-day perspective?

"The primary challenge faced by mezzanine investors is deal origination. There is a lot of capital targeting very few opportunities. Once a potential transaction has been identified, day-to-day tasks are similar to those of other lenders and investors... negotiation of terms, due diligence, documentation, monitoring existing investments and so on."

What makes a good or bad mezzanine lender?

"A bad mezzanine investor takes equity risk for mezzanine returns. With essentially capped upside, it is critical that a mezzanine investor avoid capital loss. An equity investor has the potential for homerun returns, which can hide capital losses from other investments. Mezzanine investors generally do not."

Who enjoys or dislikes mezzanine lending?

"As mezzanine is primarily a credit product, a mezzanine investor needs to be more focussed on risk analysis than upside analysis. This may not be as exciting as venture capital or pure equity investing. Mezzanine investing requires one to be more aggressive than a commercial banker and more conservative than an equity investor."

Job Ideas
BMO Capital Corp (Toronto, Calgary) www.nesbittburns.com
CCFL (Toronto, Montreal) www.ccfl.com
CIBC Capital Partners (Toronto) www.cibcwm.com
Edgestone (Toronto, Montreal) www.edgestone.com
HSBC Capital (Toronto Vancouver) www.hsbc.ca
McKenna Gale (Toronto) www.mckennagale.com
Penfund (Toronto) www.penfund.com
Roynat/Scotia (offices throughout Canada) www.roynat.com
TD Capital (Toronto) www.tdcapital.com
Norvest (Toronto, Montreal) www.norvestcapital.com

Section V. Trading

9. Trading

Trading is the business of buying and selling specific financial instruments for profit or commission. A trader can be a relatively unfree, salaried, execution-based employee ("buy this, sell that"); a comparatively unfettered, profit-participating, semi-autonomous entrepreneur ("buy what you want, make a profit and we'll share the upside"); an independent; or something in between. Just about anything can be 'traded' in this sense: stocks, options on stocks, money market instruments, bonds, currency, mortgage-backed securities, asset-backed securities (e.g. credit card receivables), derivatives (futures, options, forwards), swaps. Some markets are exchange-based (e.g. stocks, options, some bonds); others are over-the-counter (e.g. bonds, swaps). Some are hyper-liquid (e.g. shares in IBM, US government bonds). Others are very illiquid (e.g. virtually any new product immediately following its inception, like mortgage-backeds two decades ago). In a liquid market, 10 large trades (or more) can be executed by a single trader in ten minutes. In an illiquid market, there may be one trade per week. Some traders have fairly quantitative, almost contemplative duties. These traders focus on analyzing the complex cash flows that constitute their instruments in order to correctly price them for clients and their own firm's needs. Other traders are operating so quickly that it is instinct and not dispassionate reason that gives them their edge. Regardless of the instrument or its liquidity, having people who know how to buy and sell a given instrument efficiently, how to quote it correctly and quickly, and where to find it are the keys to trading. That key personified is the trader.

From an economic point of view, the main point of trading is to join 'end-users' with one another. In the simplest case, the owner of 100 shares who is planning to sell them wants to be able to find a buyer. Brokers exist to serve these two clients and the brokers use traders to execute the trade mechanically. ('Used' might be the better term here. Such a simple transaction is more and more likely to be done electronically, although brokerage firms still aggregate their orders through a human trader.) Think of the old stock exchange floor. To do this trade, two traders would actually meet and do the 100-share trade, evidenced by paper. A large thrust of the large firms' efforts are aimed at serving clients in the same way. The needs of a billion-dollar-a-year exporter may be more complex than those of the 100-share shareholder, but the task is theoretically the same. Who can be found who will sell the exporter-client the required amount of currency forwards? The firm defines the need, finds the right counterparty (or his trader), executes the trade and pockets a commission (or marks up the initial price and resells the instrument for a small profit).

That all worked fine until the firms in a given field started noticing that they had enough information to speculate on supply and demand and on prices. It became interesting for them to hold inventory of certain instruments so that they had the product on the shelf when the client called or so they could speculate on the price and make a profit quite apart from the needs of their actual clients. The modern profession of trading was born.

As a result, you will find many traders engaging in

both kinds of trading simultaneously. They will take positions in products to speculate on price or on the future needs of their clients. (Remember a position can be a short one, so if prices are forecast to go down, the trader can still profit.) They will close out those positions to lock in gains or limit losses. They will also go out and find a given product solely because a given client needs it.

In the world of stocks, there is a distinction made between 'pro' and liability trading. Pro trading is purely self-interested. If a stock is forecast to go up, buy it. When it has done (or not done) its thing, sell it. There is no reference to any client needs or corporate goals. Liability trading is more of a hybrid between agency and pro trading. The trader is very much an employee of the firm in question and is directed toward certain instruments. The goal is to take positions for profit, but only target the instruments of issuers about which the firm has a reputation as a dealer. An important subsidiary goal is to provide liquidity and credibility as a dealer in those instruments. Being in and out on a daily basis helps build that credibility.

When it comes to working in this field, the choice of firms and jobs is vast. Different size firms, different instruments, different type of trading. I would recommend looking at the intern programs of the large banks. These programs rotate the trainees through many different departments before offering (or not offering) them a particular posting. Whether the big bank route is for you or not, the exposure can't hurt.

Culture

I've found the traders that I've met to be informal, gregarious and extremely focussed on their discipline.

They dress informally. They have shorter hours than most other professions covered here. They love to joke, especially at someone's else's expense. They swear. Some burp. They are sometimes inactive for hours on end. But when there is action in their market, they become deadly serious, focussed and tough. If you're slow to catch on (to concepts or jokes) or take 'razzing' badly, I can't imagine you're going to have much fun or success in the trading environment. On the negative side, they often know little about other professions – even other types of trading. A trader once asked me what 'comps' were – and he worked on the same floor as investment bankers. In addition, they have high stress jobs and can burn out early without a clear alternative career path. Technology is also a threat to some trading jobs.

Trading

André Charbonneau

Education:
BA, University of Montreal (1965)
BComm, HEC (University of Montreal) (1969)
WEP, University of Western Ontario (1990)

Experience:
Junior Trader (currency trading), RBC – Montreal (1970-1972)
Trader (currency trading), RBC – NY, London (1972-73)
Chief Trader & Treasurer (currency trading/bonds), RBC – Paris (1973-1977)
Business development, RBC – Montreal (1977-1981)
Chief Trader Foreign currencies, RBC – Toronto (1981-1985)
Treasurer, Treasury, RBC – London (1985-1987)
VP, Treasury-Québec, RBC – Montreal (1987-1994)
VP, Gestion Privée TAL – Montreal (1994-2001)

Current job:
Retired.

How would you describe the function of a trader in the financial world? Why does this profession and set of responsibilities exist in this way?

"The trader's function in the financial market is to manage risk and create value. The function exists because corporations are now operating in a global market where everything is a commodity, i.e. resources, currencies, interest rates, and are thus at risk of seeing the value of the goods or services it produces to fluctuate as it is marked to market."

How would you describe the job of a trader from a mechanical and day-to-day perspective?
"There are at least four different types of traders:

(1) proprietary traders, i.e. those trading/speculating for a corporation's own account;

(2) hedgers, whose main purpose is to minimize risk by covering exposures;

(3) arbitrageurs, who will seek transactions where they can make a profit without taking risk;

(4) corporate traders, who work inside financial institutions and are more sales people who will seek to do transactions with clients."

What makes a good or bad trader?
"A good trader is one that has confidence in his own analysis, acts accordingly and recognizes quickly when the market view is different... A bad trader is someone who marries his positions or who does not know when to cut his losses."

Who enjoys or dislikes trading?
"People who enjoy very short-term results, the flow of adrenaline, fast action and living on edge will enjoy trading. People who do not enjoy pressure should avoid it."

Trading in a sentence:
"The greatest job there is!"

Annie Bergevin

Education:
Civil Engineering Degree, McGill University (1996)
CFA designation, AIMR (1999)
MBA, Columbia University (2001)

Experience:
Manager, mortgage trading, MCAP Financial – Toronto (1997-9)
Investment banking, CSFB – New York (2001-3)

Current job:
Financial and strategic consulting.

How would you describe the function of a trader in the financial world? Why does this profession and set of responsibilities exist in this way?

"The function of a trader is to match investor's requests with the right products. It is his job to find the best price and the right quantity for his clients. A trader keeps the market very efficient and transparent. He knows where products are at all times and knows who wants to sell and who wants to buy. Speed is key in this profession."

How would you describe the job of a trader from a mechanical and day-to-day perspective?

"First thing in the morning, I would read the macro economic news. Interest rates and their potential movement are very important to the mortgage market. Then, I would look to see what commitments (mortgages not yet funded) had come through the pipeline the night before. Based on my client's needs, I would allocate these commitments.

Then, I managed a $25 million funded mortgage portfolio that was owned by my company (proprietary trading). I would hedge the portfolio against interest rate risk (I shorted bonds with similar duration as the mortgages).

Then, probably once a week, I would package these mortgages and sell them as a portfolio to institutional investors. I would price these portfolios based on same maturity government bonds and add a spread depending on how risky the portfolio was. Also, 3-4 times a year, we would issue CMHC-insured MBS (mortgage-backed securities). This was done through investment dealers."

What makes a good or bad trader?

"For trading, you need to be good with numbers and see patterns quickly. You need to have a good memory to know who owns what for block trades and have good social skills with clients."

Who enjoys or dislikes trading?

"You need to like high stress, as well as a fast-paced and exciting environment. People are usually outgoing and loud. If you like to analyze companies in depth and understand their business models, this is not the job for you."

In a sentence:

"High stress, high reward"

Patrick Houston

Education:
BA (Religious Studies), Mount Allison University (1997)
NASD Series 7 Registered representative (2000)

Current job:
Arbitrage, spread, 'momentum' and 'scalping' trader for personal account (NYSE, NASDAQ listed stocks) – Montreal (1999-)

How would you describe the function of a trader in the financial world? Why does this profession and set of responsibilities exist in this way?

"Day trading exists because of technology. NASDAQ is a good example of technology's relationship with trading. The NASDAQ has no trading floor, and no specialists matching orders manually. The entire market place is digital and is displayed with automated quotes (AQ). Advances in technology such as these have made the world of trading accessible to everyone with an internet connection. These new traders impact volatility and liquidity because they introduce volume combined with instant execution capabilities. It is no longer a world of giant institutional buying and selling: it is the mother who finds she has a knack for trading, and the college grad who doesn't want a boss. Being able to trade online, therefore, brings the market closer to the notion of it being public, and skips the expensive, and often ineffective stock broker whose self interests tend to leave the investor asking 'what happened?'"

How would you describe the job of a trader from a mechanical and day-to-day perspective?

"Many trades are placed throughout the day with the intention of capitalizing in seconds or hours. Due to the prolific trading nature of day trading, fundamentals play very little part in decisions, and analysis plays a very important one."

What makes a good or bad trader?

"Good traders know their limitations. Bad traders think they can outsmart the market…Never works."

Who enjoys or dislikes trading?

"Trading is not for everyone. It is a career that might leave some people wondering if they have created anything of value other than monetarily. Unless one advances technologies or strategies in the trading world, there is no 'body of work' to look back on upon retirement. On the other hand there is a sense of accomplishment that comes with being self-employed along with the benefits it brings with it. So it is certainly a personal choice as to what an individual is searching for in a career."

Trading in a sentence:

"A video game that features a massive swirling pool mixed with money, and the objective is to put your hand in at the right time to claim your prize."

Job Ideas

Trading is a VAST profession. As noted above, any security (e.g. stocks, bonds, options, future, forwards, swaps, currency, commodities) can be traded on an agency or principal basis. Banks (in a number of ways and in a number of distinct departments), investment dealers, money managers, pension and mutual funds, specialized firms (e.g. in commodities and foreign exchange) and large companies all need traders. What follows are just SOME ideas.

The Banks & Their Investment Dealers
Bank of Montreal/BMO www.nesbittburns.com or
   www4.bmo.com
Bank of Nova Scotia/Scotia Bank www.scotiacapital.com or
   www.scotiabank.com/
CIBC www.cibcwm.com or www.cibc.com
Desjardins www.vmd.ca or www.desjardins.com
Laurentian www.vmbl.ca or www.laurentianbank.com
National Bank www.nbfinancial.com or www.nbc.ca
Royal Bank of Canada/RBC www.rbccm.com or
   www.rbc.com
TD www.tdsecurities.com or www.td.com

The Investment Dealers
Brant Securities (Toronto) www.brantsec.com
Canaccord (Toronto, Montreal, Calgary and Vancouver plus
   branches across Canada) www.canaccord.com
Casgrain & Company (Montreal) 514.871.8080
First Associates/Rockwater (Toronto) www.firstassociates.com
GMP Securities (Toronto, Montreal and Calgary)
   www.gmpsecurities.com
Haywood Securities (Vancouver, Calgary and Toronto)
   www.haywood.com
Loewen, Ondaatje, McCutcheon (Toronto) www.lomltd.com
Maison Placements (Toronto) www.maisonplacements.com

Northern Securities (Toronto, Vancouver and Calgary) www.northernsi.com
Orion (Toronto, Montreal and Calgary) www.orionsecurities.ca
Peters & Co. (Calgary) www.petersco.com
Research Capital (Toronto, Montreal, Calgary and Vancouver plus branches across Ontario) www.researchcapital.com
Sprott Securities (Toronto, Montreal and Calgary) www.sprott.ca

The Funds

Beutel, Goodman & Company Ltd. (Toronto) www.beutel-can.com
BIMCOR – Bell's pension fund (Montreal) 514.394.4750
Bluewater (Toronto) 416-599-5300
Burgundy (Toronto and Montreal) www.burgundy-asset.com
Caisse/Caisse de dépôt et placement du Québec (Montreal, Quebec City) www.lacaisse.com
CI Mutual Funds Inc. (Toronto) www.cifunds.com
Co-operators Investment Counselling Limited (Guelph) www.cooperatorsinvestment.ca
CPP (Canada Pension Plan) Investment Board (Toronto) www.cppib.ca
Cundill Investment Research Ltd. (Vancouver) www.cundill.com
Dundee Wealth Management (Toronto) www.dundeewealth.com
AGF Management Limited (Toronto) www.agf.com
Gluskin Sheff + Associates Inc. (Toronto) www.gluskinsheff.com
Goodman and Company Investment Counsel see Dundee Wealth Management
Greystone Capital Management Inc. (Regina) (306) 779-6400
Gryphon (Toronto, Montreal and Halifax) www.gryphon.ca
Howson Tattersall (Toronto) htic.ca
HSBC Asset Management (Toronto, Montreal, Vancouver, Calgary) www.hsbc.ca
Jarislowsky Fraser (Toronto, Montreal and Calgary) www.jfl.ca

Jones Heward/Bank of Montreal (Toronto, Calgary) www.jonesheward.com
McLean Budden (Toronto, Montreal and Vancouver) www.mcleanbudden.com
Montrusco Bolton (Montreal, Quebec, Toronto, Calgary, Halifax, Moncton) www.montruscobolton.com
Natcan/National Bank (Montreal) www.natcan.com
OMERS/Ontario Municipal Employees Retirement System (Toronto) www.omers.com
Phillips, Hager & North (Toronto, Montreal, Vancouver, Calgary and Victoria) www.phn.com
Pictet (Montreal) 514.288.8161
RBC Asset Management Inc /Royal Bank www.rbcam.com
Scotia Cassels/Bank of Nova Scotia (Toronto) www.scotiacassels.com
TAL/CIBC (Toronto and Montreal) www.tal.ca
TD Asset Management www.tdassetmanagement.com
Teachers/Ontario Teachers' Pension Plan (Toronto) www.otpp.com

Part D: Some Practical Points

1. A Note on the CFA

I completed the three exams of the CFA and was awarded the CFA charter in 2003. I then let it lapse given my new publishing career – hence the absence of the letters 'CFA' after my name. I can honestly say that it was one of the most unfun experiences of my life and tarnished my previous positive feeling about springtime. (The exams were always on June 1 or thereabouts, so for three years in a row, spring was severely compromised by studying.) That being said, I don't regret it.

People considering it, though, should know what it's about. Firstly, it is very well regarded, so all the sweat is worth it. Secondly, the content is very statistical. The course is not for the innumerate or for individuals who like to go by instinct or gut. Thirdly and perhaps most importantly, it is very money manager-focussed and, to a lesser extent, equity analyst-focussed. I've known a lot of investment, corporate and merchant bankers who have taken it, but it does not address their specific professions. Some topics (e.g. private equity/merchant banking, venture capital, mezzanine, real estate) get a reading or two on one exam (of three total), whereas public company investing, bond trading, derivatives and portfolio structuring (and don't forget statistics) are tested *ad nauseam* over all three exams. My guess is that non-money managers have to work harder as a result. Even if a money manager has only one, very specific expertise that he knows well and even if he begins the CFA program when he is just starting out in the profession, by exams 2 and 3 he should be able to go through significant parts of the material extremely quickly because of his work experience. I can't say the same for merchant and investment bankers. Trust me, I was one.

Should you do it? We live in a credentialist world and every piece of paper counts, but, on the other hand, *sed fugit interea, fugit irreparabile tempus* ('time flies, never to return') and money doesn't grow on trees (if you're paying for the course yourself).

As ever, my advice is simple: be informed.

2. A Note on Financial Ratios, Statements & Pro Formas

In almost all financial fields, a lot of time is spent analyzing ratios and financial statements. The vocabulary can become quite abstruse. (I often find, by the way, that people use arcane terms either to intimidate people or because they don't know what they are talking about themselves.) As in all other matters, my guide is here to help. Here are few terms demystified.

LTM

LTM stands for 'last twelve months' and has evolved in the quest for the most up-to-date information on companies. Public companies only report whole years of financial data once a year (and this data is way too old to be informative by months 9, 10 or 11 of the next year), but they do report quarterly data for the three quarters following a year end. Financial ratios, on the other hand, are all based either on moment-in-time balance sheet items and/or a *full year* of financial data. As a result, users of financial data tend to take the last full year of financial results; add the reported, post-year end quarters and subtract the oldest quarters included in the year end results in order to come up with 'LTM' historical data. While future-oriented financial information is best from a theoretical point of view (who cares what a company has done in the past?), it is also hard to come by and, of course, imperfect. (Strangely enough, don't be surprised to hear people talk about projections as though they are sure to happen. I have seen both financial people and operators do this. I have also rarely heard of projections actually being accurate. Don't ask me.)

On the other hand, don't be surprised if people spend a lot of time on past performance. *Theoretically*, the past is irrelevant to valuation, to lending decisions etc ... – unless there are lawsuits or other hidden liabilities as a result of past activities. Nevertheless, the past is important in a lot of contexts. Firstly, it speaks to credibility. In merchant banking, we often met with management teams who confidently predicted impressive growth from the moment of our involvement and despite years of flatlining. We called this sudden change the 'hockey stick'. (Don't say Canada hasn't contributed to the vocabulary of finance.) When it was the same management team for both periods, we often asked: "Why is the prospect today so different from the prospect of 3 years ago *as it actually turned out to be*?" There was often silence, and a credibility gap. Secondly, for slow growth or no growth companies (there are more of these than financial-types like to admit), the future and the past aren't so different. If a company did $100 million of revenue last year, it is very likely to do $98 or $105 this year. Even what happened three years ago might be relevant.

As a result of all these factors, a lot of time is spent on LTM analysis. (Always looking at a full year, of course, also eliminates any seasonality the company may be subject to.)

Forwards

A forward multiple is a ratio computed using an income statement or cash flow figure that is a projection – often now introduced by the phrase 'going forward'. In 2005, an example would be a PE ratio based on today's stock price, but using the earnings projected for 2006 (usually called '2006E' or '2006F'). Often, these figures go out more than one year, e.g. price/earnings 2006E = 5.9x, price/earnings 2007E = 3.7x. (Note that, since most projections show rising profits, the multiples tend to go down as the projection period lengthens. Checking for this fall-off is a quick way to proof read lists of multiples. In practice, results don't trend upwards so nicely, but whatever.)

Forwards can be very handy. For instance, if a firm has past losses, but projected profits (they often do), the forwards give people a non-negative (i.e. meaningful) figure to work with. Also, if the past numbers are 'dirty' (see below), the forwards can give a clean picture of the company.

Historical numbers are often 'dirty' due to acquisitions (or asset sales) that closed mid-fiscal year. Since everyone wants an income statement or cash flow number that represents the company's *potential profitability* **today** (even if the numbers that represent that potential profitability come from the past), numbers that have only the partial contribution of subsidiaries that are now a part of the company are incomplete or 'dirty'. (Sometimes, past numbers can be adjusted to make them complete – see *Pro Forma* below.) The forward numbers are 'clean' because the forecaster will include (or should include) the results of all currently owned subsidiaries in his projections. In general, investment bankers tend to prefer LTM numbers (because they can be obtained from publicly available information without anybody but the investment bankers themselves knowing) and equity analysts prefer forwards (because forecasting goes to the core of their job and as people who cover companies day-in, day-out, they have the company- and industry-specific knowledge to make the forecasts themselves).

Pro Forma

I have never used Latin more than during my time in investment banking. Unfortunately, it was only two words of that language: *pro forma*. Numbers can be *pro forma*-ed six ways to Sunday. Basically, the idea behind *pro forma*s is to clean up 'dirty' numbers so as to have numbers that indeed represent the reality behind a given fact or potential event. (In a quite different context, *pro forma* can also be used as a fancy term for 'projections' or 'estimates'.)

One main kind of *pro forma* is the revised historical result. If a company has bought or sold a company or division, the past results are no longer indicative of what the company can do **today**. Sometimes, the information exists to adjust the historical numbers so that a hypothetical set of results can be created for the past, i.e. what the company *would have* looked like if the acquisitions of the past year had been done before the year began. In the case of a purchase, the adjusted results will be higher than the reported ones; in the case of an asset sale, lower. Sometimes, the balance sheet or capital structure will also have to be adjusted – e.g. if a debt or equity issue has closed after the reported balance sheet – although this is less frequent because public companies report new balance sheets every quarter. The quarterly balance sheet and share structure will catch the financing effect of the new acquisition or divestiture even when the unadjusted/reported LTM income statement won't.

Another frequent *pro forma* is the forward-looking one. In this case, the goal is to look at what two companies *would look like* if they *were* to merge. This is very frequently done in the mergers and acquisitions field. If a given merger is being pitched to a prospective client, the buyer will want to know what the merged company will look like. The *pro forma* can tell the story. The investment bankers will often want to add some spice to the picture by adding projected synergies (i.e. identified savings from bringing the two companies together) to the *pro forma* results.

EBITDA

EBITDA means earnings before interest, taxes, depreciation and amortization. (EBIT, more often used in the past, means earnings before interest and taxes.) EBITDA is ubiquitous. I have heard people say that it ought not be. There are legitimate criticisms of EBITDA. EBITDA is not free cash flow that can be spent as one wishes. It is not earnings against which all cash and non-cash costs have been charged. It is not perfect. Nevertheless, after five years in finance working on companies in many industries (e.g. retail, printing, packaging, steel, telecom, media, auto parts), it is the undoubtedly the undisputed queen of the profitability measurements. Learn to love it.

Why is EBITDA so used? I think the key to its popularity is its relative usefulness, simplicity and stability. EBITDA is useful because it is a 'cash flow-y' type figure. EBITDA is what a company would make in cash if it were paid cash for all its products, paid cash to all its suppliers and paid no taxes or interest. As such, it gives some idea of the financial strength of the company. EBITDA is also relatively simple. Increasingly, it can be calculated by examining just the income statement. Perhaps most importantly, EBITDA is stable. For a mature and stable company, EBITDA (and EBITDA margins) from year to year will be relatively constant – hopefully growing, but not wildly different from year to year. It is thus a good measurement to watch for trends, for financial strength, for comparison between companies etc ...

Many other contending figures do not have these characteristics. For instance, earnings are not as useful, simple or stable. Earnings may be affected downward (and correctly) by the notional 'using up' of long-term assets, but this lower figure understates the company's resources in any given year – i.e. it will often make more cash than that. Earnings are not simple either. The man (or journalist) on the street may say that companies should only report their 'true', bottom line earnings, but most people can't easily grasp the idea of non-cash expenses (especially not amortization – to whatever extent it still exists). Earnings are not stable either: tax rates can vary and write-downs/accounting gains affect them. Another contender, free cash flow, is theoretically what all financial providers want (i.e. free cash to pay off debt and pay dividends to shareholders), but, when used from a single year of results, it has faults, too. Firstly, swings in the working capital accounts (receivables, payables, inventory) can provide or use up cash at a single point in time without meaning anything profound about a company's ability to generate cash. (Such swings can also warn of a coming apocalypse, but that's another story.) Secondly, free cash flow includes capital expenditures and these outlays can be enormous in one year and tiny the next. As a result, free cash flow is not stable like EBITDA.

All this to say that, theoretically there are better measurements and ideally all measurements will be examined over multi-year periods, but EBITDA as the most used measurement is probably here to stay. Learn to love it.

(In terms of analyzing companies, I think that too little thought has been put into the natural life cycle of companies, i.e. of looking at what happens to expenses, capex and off balance sheet liabilities over multi-year periods. It seems to me that a company in its 20th year of operation is categorically different from a startup – even if they are in the same field – just as a seasonal company examined in the wintertime is different from one examined in the summer. All sorts of 'plaque' builds up inside old companies: union agreements with ratchets, pension liabilities, environmental costs etc … Accountants and financial types may try to characterize these things quickly and numerically in footnotes to financial statements or via due diligence, but it seems to be that there is 'life cycle' analysis that is missing in the theory and obscured by the exclusive focus on monthly, quarterly or yearly analysis. These costs build up and show up over years – and only a longer focus period can properly catch them. To be more concrete: a financial type will usually look at a perennial cost and project its evolution into the future by increasing it by inflation. In fact, its path may follow a very different course.)

For brief definitions of EBITDAR and EBITDAM, see the Glossary.

Enterprise Value

Many financial ratios do not use the equity value of a company as the numerator, but instead use 'enterprise value' or 'total enterprise value' or, when you really get to know him well, 'TEV'. Enterprise value is simply the sum of a company's debt and equity values. It is necessary to use enterprise value when working with EBITDA, because unlike earnings, EBITDA 'belongs' to both the debt and equity holders. For this reason, the multiple to be computed with EBITDA must relate to the value of all the financial stakeholders – even if some of these stakeholders (i.e. the lenders) have a fixed payoff.

DCFs

You will learn in school that the best way to value a company is the 'DCF' (discounted cash flow). You may be surprised to learn that many large investors will not even build such a model, much less use it to value a company. They will invest off multiples and projections, but leave the DCF in the textbooks. Why?

(For those unfamiliar with DCFs, the idea is to find out what the future dollars to be earned by a company are worth today. The less you pay today for future dollars, the greater your return. For instance, if you want to make a 10% return, you should pay $1 for the ability to receive $1.10 a year from now. If you pay more than a $1, your return will be less. If you pay less, your return will be greater. An investor should demand a greater return (and pay less) for riskier situations. A DCF discounts all the future dollars a company is projected to make. Of course, not all future dollars to infinity can in fact be projected. This limitation has nothing to do with the quality of projections, just the mechanical impossibility of projecting an infinite series of discrete numbers. For this reason, after the first set of forecast years – often five years – the modeller must do a simplified calculation to value the company's perpetuity – i.e. the value of all the future dollars past the five year projection period.)

I can't speak for all the non-users of DCFs, but I know that all the DCFs that I worked on were nonsense. Why? Simply put, too much of the value in a DCF comes from the perpetuity. The first five years of 'true' projections do not even contribute 50% to the computed company or enterprise value. As you know, once the discount rate and final projected cash flow have been determined, the perpetuity value is a function of the terminal growth rate. Try guessing what the growth rate of a company will be in five years time for the period starting at that moment and ending in 'infinity'. To make it even more ridiculous, the perpetuity's value is very sensitive to small changes in that growth rate. A 0.2% difference will make millions of dollars difference. End result: the value of the company is whatever you want it to be – and, in fact, the value generated by the DCF will always *be made* to equal or come close to what (1) the value *already is* (for, say, a public company); or (2) what the public market multiples from the relevant industry imply when applied to the company in question's results; or (3) what the bidder is bidding. Of course, market multiples (unlike discount rates) don't have any inherent meaning, so the exercise is circular. Multiples come from the market to determine asset prices which in turn imply multiples which determine market prices.

(One could look at DCFs in other way. Given a market price or a price implied by market multiples, building a DCF *that results in that same price* gives you a scenario that fleshes out at least one set of underlying parameters – i.e. growth, cash flow etc ... – that goes with that value. If you are assessing a bid and the DCF needs unrealistically high growth rates in order to reach the bid price, it might a signal to sell – and vice versa as a bidder.)

(By the way, it seems to me that other areas of

finance are circular too. Take beta. A stock's sensitivity to the whole market gives it a beta. That beta implies a cost to its equity that will theoretically be used in a DCF to come up with a stock price. But swings in the company's *stock price* were needed to compute its beta in the first place. On what basis were those valuation changes made? The same is true for the market as a whole. What if there were no market, how would we value equity?)

Of course, DCFs rely on projections. Since projections can be utter nonsense, the underlying DCF can be nonsense for that reason, too.

(By the way, anyone who believes that big companies take everything they do very seriously and scientifically should consider this story. As an investment banker, I worked on a valuation mandate of a largish public company. When we asked how the price for a joint venture partner's stake in a related company had been calculated, we were told that some cock-and-bull story about how much the seller's *grandmother* was going to pay for his shares had formed the negotiating base line!)

3. Microsoft Excel

Excel is your friend. Most of the disciplines here make at least some use of it. Many use it extensively and many entry-level professionals will spend most of their time on Excel models.

Learn as much as you can about Excel. Back in 1999, I spent about $50 for *Using Microsoft Excel 97* by Ron Person. It was a great investment. It showed me how to save all sorts of time and do things that are not obvious. My advice? Learn! Learn about using dollar signs to keep rows and columns constant. Learn how to record macros and turn them into buttons. Learn how to customize your buttons. Learn about sensitivity tables. (Higher-ups love sensitivity tables.) Learn about formatting options. Learn about different ways to copy and paste material (formatting, values only etc ...). Learn about 'F4'. Everything you can do to make things be clearer and go faster will be valuable. Doing it now (while you're still in school) might save you precious hours of sleep in the near future.

At the same time, don't treat Excel like a magic machine. The old adage about 'garbage in, garbage out' is 100% true. The hardest thing about modelling is not the theoretical stuff. (The occasional theoretical problems that I encountered tended to be swept under the carpet or sidestepped by the higher-ups.) The hardest thing is entering hundreds of numbers and equations without making simple, stupid, but material, errors.

Here is some more advice:

Design your Excel models to be proofed on paper. Even though you can input large equations into a single cell, don't. If there are five variables in an equation, use six cells, so you can see all the variables *and* the result without having to 'go into' a cell. It takes up more space, but you'll find errors faster. Don't put any important information anywhere where it will not be visible when printed.

Proof on paper. Use a pocket calculator to proof your (printed) models. What is not obvious on the computer screen can become so when it is on paper and checked by hand.

Proof tables. Even if you trust your model, don't trust your sensitivity tables. There can an error in the model that only manifests itself in the tables. Read the tables to make sure they make sense. Fiddle with the model on your computer or with two printed versions to test the results of the tables.

Try to get other people to proof your models. Another set of eyes always helps. Despite the wisdom of such a practice, I found higher-ups generally uninterested in having it done. Try.

Do reality checks. If a number seems odd, break it down to justify it or find the error.

Make everything dynamic. Don't embed numbers (hard codes) in equations. Firstly, some mucky-muck is going to want to vary that variable. Secondly, if there is an error, hardcoding will keep you from finding it.

Build in equational proofs. Use Excel to proof Excel. The simplest example of this practice is the balance sheet 'footing', i.e. the right hand minus the left hand should equal zero. There are a lot of other tests you can build in. Calculate a single result two ways and make sure the numbers are equal.

In the case of simple tasks, do the whole thing twice. I used to do this with 'comps' (see Chapter 1, "Investment Banking" in The Guide below). It took

1.5 times as long, but I (sometimes) caught errors before the material got used.

Input inputted numbers down to the last penny. This makes it easy to retrace where certain numbers (or wrong numbers or typos) came from.

Proof again.

A (Short) Glossary of Terms

Ask. The price at which a seller is willing to sell a financial instrument.

Bid. The price at which a buyer is willing to buy a financial instrument.

Company. In this book, an operating company (as opposed to a financial *firm*).

Comps. Comparables. Companies in a given industry that are deemed 'comparable'. Ideally, they will be in exactly the same industry, the same size, the same nationality etc ... In practice (especially in Canada), they are often only in the same general field (e.g. 'retailing').

Commercial banking. Generically, the business of lending money (versus other kinds of 'banking', e.g. investment banking). Specifically, at many Canadian banks, bank-to-company lending with a low dollar threshold, e.g. under $20 million.

Corporate banking. Bank-to-company lending. Usually with a high dollar threshold ($20+ million).

DCF. Discounted cash flow. Nowadays, almost always an Excel model of a company's future financial results. The purpose is to find out what the free cash flows of the company are and then discount them (i.e. give them a value in today's dollars) using the company's WACC or cost of equity. DCF's can be leveraged or unleveraged.

EBIT. Earnings before interest and taxes.

EBITDA. Earnings before interest, taxes, depreciation and amortization.

EBITDAM. Earnings before interest, taxes, depreciation, amortization and marketing. This is a useful internal metric for companies that are growing fast and spending wildly on marketing to grow their market share before (the theory goes) that market either consolidates or becomes more stable. EBITDAM might be positive (and so show a company that *could* be profitable) when EBITDA is negative (due to purportedly medium-term factors).

EBITDAR. Earnings before interest, taxes, depreciation, amortization and rent. This measurement is used for companies that rent so many assets that leasing is replacing debt capital as a financing device. The capital structure and EBITDA of these companies is distorted because instead of borrowing money and buying necessary assets, they lease them and pay EBITDA-lowering rent. Just as pre-interest EBITDA goes with enterprise value (i.e. the sum of equity *and* debt values), EBITDAR has to be associated with an enterprise value adjusted to include the value of the rented assets.

Enterprise value. The sum of a company's equity value and debt.

Firm. In this book, a financial firm (as opposed to an operating *company*).

Forward. A financial ratio calculated off of a projected number.

I-banker. Investment banker.

IB. Investment banking.

LQA. Last quarter annualized.

LTM. Last twelve months.

M&A. Mergers and acquisitions.

Offer. The price at which a seller is willing to sell a financial instrument.

OSC. The Ontario Securities Commission. The securities regulator of Ontario and *de facto* securities regulator of Canada.

PE. Price/earnings ratio. Also, private equity.

Precedent transaction. A previously executed sale of a whole company, the multiples from which are used a benchmark for future transactions in the industry.

Pro forma. Financial data that has somehow been modified to account for some past or future/hypothetical event. Also, another term for projections.

SEC. The Securities and Exchange Commission. The US securities regulator.

Secondary issue. *Meaning 1:* the sale of a very large block of shares in a public company by a shareholder. A sale of this size will usually require a prospectus. *Meaning 2:* a subsequent issue of shares from treasury by an already-public company.

Underwriting. The business of bringing securities to market, traditionally by owning them for a (hopefully) short period of time.

VC. Venture capital or venture capitalist.

IA (Very Select) Bibliography

Business people generally do not go in much for history, nor, I might also add, for the theoretical underpinnings of a market-driven, capitalist society. In both cases, it is a shame. As the Ecclesiastes tells us, "There is no new thing under the sun." Financial mania, overleveraging, overlending, conflicts of interest – they are all *perennial*. If you want to understand more about these things, I recommend these books:

Brooks, John. *The Go-Go Years: The Drama and Crashing Finale of Wall Street's Bullish 1960's.* Allworth Press, 1973.

Burrough, Bryan and Helyar, John. *Barbarians at the Gate: The Fall of RJR Nabisco.* Harper Perennial, 1990.

Fay, Stephen. *Beyond Greed: The Hunt Family's Bold Attempt to Corner the Silver Market.* Penguin Books: New York, 1982.

Ferris, Paul. *Gentlemen of Fortune.* Weidenfeld and Nicolson: London, 1984.

Rothchild, John. *Going for Broke: How Robert Campeau Bankrupted the Retail Industry, Jolted the Junk Bond Market, and Brought the Booming 80s to a Crashing Halt.* Beard Books, 2000.

Lewis, Michael. *Liar's Poker.* Penguin Books, 1989.

Schwed, Jr., Fred. *Where are the Customers' Yachts?* John Wiley & Sons, Inc., 1940.

Account executives, 91
Accountant(s), 18, 46, 102, 138, 150, 179
Accounting, 31-32, 43, 139, 145, 178, 190
Accounts receivable SEE RECEIVABLES
Active investing, 111-112
Analyst(s), 12, 35-36, 40-41, 50, 52, 54, 59-66, 64-66, 68-69, 82, 118, 124, 130, 175
Angel investors, 126
Anti-trust, 46
Asian meltdown, 20
Associate(s), 54, 58, 62, 64, 65, 68, 70, 82, 106, 122-123, 130, 144, 154, 168-169
Audit, 31-32, 102
Auto parts, 75, 177
Back office, 17
Balance sheet, 43, 72, 148, 150, 173, 176, 179, 184
Bank mergers, 20
Bank of Canada, 48
Bank of Montreal, 57, 70, 72, 86, 88, 121, 150, 168, 170
Bankers' acceptances, 91
Bankruptcy, 74, 77
BComm, 9, 62, 102, 114, 118, 140, 144, 162
Bell, 18, 121, 132, 169
Beneficiary(ies), 26-29, 90
Benvest, 123
Beta, 182
'Big five' banks, 72
BMO, 57, 64, 70, 72, 86, 88, 106, 147, 150, 156, 168
Board of directors, 30, 80
Bonds, 78, 81, 91, 96, 105, 157, 162, 165, 168
Bonus(es), 9, 31-32, 60
Book (of clients), 91, 94, 104
Branch, 13, 22-23, 57, 70, 86
Bubble, 12
Buffet, Warren, 98
Burns Fry, 88

Buyouts, 16, 136, 140, 144, 148, 151
Caisse, 54, 72, 82, 87, 107, 109, 121, 140, 147, 169
Calgary, 11, 40, 57-58, 70-71, 86-87, 106, 121-122, 147, 156, 168-170
Canada Pension Plan, 109, 121, 169
Canada's Venture Capital & Private Equity Association, 135, 147
Canadian Securities Course, 92
Canadian Western Bank, 72, 86, 88
Capital expenditures/capex, 32, 42, 73, 178-179
Capital structure, 176, 187
Capital tax, 43
Carried interest/carry, 17, 124
CEO, 21, 30, 32, 52, 141
CFA, 1, 7, 54, 64, 68, 82, 102, 110, 118, 130, 164, 171
CFO, 32, 52, 140
Chairman, 30
Chartered bank(s), 12, 16, 21-22, 35-36, 48, 89, 91, 95, 148
Chinese walls, 60
Churning, 109
CIBC, 57, 70, 72, 86, 88, 106, 121, 147, 150, 156, 168, 170
Clairvest, 123, 147
Commercial banking, 72, 186, 190
Commercial paper, 91
Commodity(ies), 77, 81, 103, 105, 162, 168
Compliance, 6, 34-35, 37, 96, 109, 118
Comps, 44, 160, 184, 186
Conduct and Practices Handbook Course, 92
Consultant(s), 54, 56, 130, 144
Consulting, 81, 141, 144, 164
Convertible debt, 127-128

Index

Corporate banker(s), 40, 72-73, 76-80, 82-85, 89, 95, 124-125
Corporate banking, 6, 14, 48, 72-73, 75, 77, 79-85, 87-89, 186, 190
Corporation, 26-29, 78, 132, 135, 150, 163
Cost of equity, 186
Coupon, 149
Covenant(s), 73-74, 76, 78, 83, 149, 151
Credit card, 157
Credit department, 76, 80, 89
Culture, 19-20, 46-47, 63, 77, 95, 112, 124-125, 128, 139, 149, 159
Currency, 157-158, 162, 168
CV, 10
Cynicism, 14, 96
DCF, 46, 180-182, 186, 190
Deal flow, 23, 138
Derivative(s), 80, 108, 111, 130, 157, 171
Dirty (numbers), 175-176
Dividends, 27, 98, 117, 178
Dominion Securities, 50, 52, 88, 106
Coxe, Don, 98
DOS, 93
Dot.com, 11-13, 15, 25, 29
Due diligence, 18, 33, 45, 55, 80, 84, 138-139, 151, 155, 179
Earnings, 62, 174-175, 177-179, 186-188, 190
'Eat what you kill', 105
EBIT, 62, 73, 177, 186
EBITDA, 13, 44, 62, 73, 177-180, 186-187
EBITDAM, 179, 186-187
EBITDAR, 179, 187
Edgestone, 17, 135, 147, 156
Enron, 15, 32
Enterprise value, 42-44, 179, 181, 187

Entrepreneur(s), 47-48, 93, 123, 126, 134, 141, 157
Entrepreneurial, 56, 105, 130, 151
Equity analysis, 6, 59, 61, 63, 65, 67, 69, 71
Equity analyst(s), 12, 36, 40-41, 59-65, 68-69, 124, 130, 175
Equity research, 48, 66-69
Evergreen (fund), 123
Excel, 7, 183-186
Exit, 14, 17, 138
Faber, Marc, 98
Family-controlled companies, 33
Ferris, Paul, 17, 23, 46, 48, 189
Financial engineering, 77
Financial statements, 32-33, 173, 179
First Marathon, 88
Fixed income, 103, 108-111
Fixed rate, 73
Float (of a company), 44
Floating rate, 73
Forwards (derivatives), 157-158, 168
Forwards (projections) 174-175
Four pillars, 102
Free cash flow, 25, 62, 73, 115, 177-178
Front running, 109
Fundraising, 17
Futures, 157
GAAP, 32, 43, 190
Gas, 50, 52, 63, 138
GE Capital, 72, 87
Gentlemen of Fortune, 17, 23, 46, 48, 189
Glass-Steagall Act, 51
Goldman Sachs, 51, 58
Gordon Capital, 88
Governance, 6, 30-31, 33, 37, 80
Government(s), 9, 26-7, 157, 165
Growth, 13, 25-27, 32, 55, 73, 111, 132, 174, 181

Guidance staff (at universities), 10
Halifax, 11, 57, 122, 135, 169-170
Hard code, 184
'Hockey stick', 174
Holding company discount, 45
HQ, 22
HR/human resources, 21-22, 39
Income statement, 174-177
Income trust, 6, 25-27, 29
Independent directors, 31-32
Institutional investor, 144-145
Institutional investors, 45, 59, 68, 126, 136, 148, 165
Institutional sales, 55, 61-62, 66, 94
Insurance, 51, 59, 102-103
Integration, 6, 72, 88-89
Interest rate(s), 73-74, 77, 82-83, 151, 162, 164-165
Intern program, 159
Internet, 12, 61, 166
Inventory, 75, 96, 158, 178
Investment advisor, 50, 52, 91, 96, 102
Investment banker(s), 14, 18, 36, 40, 42-48, 50-52, 54-55, 59-60, 63, 77, 89, 93, 95, 124, 138, 160, 172, 175, 177, 182, 187
Investment banking, 6, 12-14, 17, 35, 37, 39-43, 45-57, 59-62, 70, 72, 78, 80, 86, 88-89, 93-94, 96, 98, 154, 164, 176, 184, 186-187
Investment Counsel Association of Canada, 121
Investment counsellor, 107, 114
Investment Dealers' Association of Canada, 57, 70, 106
Investment Management Techniques Course, 110
Investment manager(s), 94, 107, 111-112, 132
Investment representative, 91

Investor(s), 17-18, 26-29, 36, 43, 45-46, 55, 59, 60, 66, 68, 103, 115, 123, 124, 126, 128, 131-132, 136-138, 144-145, 148, 150, 151, 154-155, 164, 165, 166, 180
IPO, 13, 37, 45, 48, 132-133
IRR, 126, 190
Jarislowsky Fraser, 108, 114, 122, 169
Journalist, 178
KKR, 18
'Know your client' rule, 92
Labour sponsored funds, 128
Laurentian, 57, 70, 72, 78, 86, 88, 106, 168
Lawsuit, 45
Lawyer(s), 18, 45-46, 138, 151
Lazard, 51, 58
LBO, 77, 136
Leasing, 43, 73, 187
Lehman Brothers, 51, 64
Lehman formula, 43
Lending, 6, 16-18, 47, 51, 72-73, 75-77, 79, 81, 83, 85, 87-89, 91, 127, 136, 152, 155, 174, 186
Leverage, 55, 77, 136-137, 186
Lewis, Michael, 19
Liability trading, 159
Liability(ies), 26-28, 109, 148, 159, 174, 179
Liar's Poker, 19, 189
Limited liability, 26, 28
Limited partnership, 28
Liquidity event, 149
Loan loss, 82-84
LQA, 13, 187
LTM, 173-176, 187
M&A, 12, 17, 42, 44-46, 51, 63, 83, 88-89, 187
Macros, 183
Management, 7, 16-17, 27-28, 30-31, 33, 35, 37, 44, 46, 66, 68-69, 78, 83-84, 88, 91, 95, 103, 107-122, 124, 130-133, 144, 150, 169-170, 174

Index

Manufacturing, 75
Market timing, 34-35
MBA, 1, 9-10, 21, 25, 62, 64, 78, 80, 82, 130, 132, 144, 150, 154, 164
McLeod Young Weir, 88
Media, 54, 177
Merchant bank (as used in England), 17
Merchant bank, 13, 15, 17-18, 125, 137, 141, 144
Merchant banker(s), 50, 77, 123, 137-138, 140-142, 144-145, 171
Mezzanine lender, 150-151, 154-155
Mezzanine, 7, 14, 16-18, 91, 123, 127, 136, 138, 148-155, 171, 190
Microcell, 17
Mid-market, 13-14
Mining, 63, 103, 138
Money management, 7, 16, 95, 107-117, 119-121
Money manager(s), 32, 37, 41, 95, 97, 107-109, 111-116, 118-120, 124, 168, 171
Money market, 91, 157
Money rental, 149
Montreal, 2, 10-13, 15, 50, 52, 54, 57-58, 64, 70-72, 78, 82, 86-88, 102, 106, 118, 121-122, 132, 135, 140, 144, 147, 150, 154, 156, 162, 166, 168-170
Mortgage-backed securities, 157, 165
Multiple, 44, 61, 174, 180, 190
Mutual fund(s), 13, 34-37, 41, 63, 68, 91, 93, 97, 103, 105, 107-109, 120-122, 168-169
National, 57, 70, 72, 78, 86, 88, 106, 121, 168, 170
Nesbitt Thomson, 88
Newco, 136-137, 148
Non-cash, 177-178
Nortel, 15, 130

NovaCap, 17, 123, 135, 144, 147
Off balance liability(ies), 179
Office of the Superintendent of Financial Institutions (OSFI), 86
Oil, 28, 50, 52, 63, 138
Old economy, 13-14
OMERS, 109, 121, 147, 170
Operating line, 14, 72, 75
Options (on treasury stock), 31,
Options (exchange traded) 157, 168
Overleverage, 75, 77, 189
Owner-operator, 137
Packaging, 177
Partnership, 16, 28
Passive investing, 111-112
Pension fund(s), 27, 41, 59, 63, 68, 90, 91, 107-108, 121, 123, 169
Perpetuity, 180-181
Person, Ron, 183
Pillars, Four, 102
PIPE, 136
Pitch, 44, 45, 47, 55, 60
Portfolio company(ies), 14, 75, 124, 127, 136, 138, 141
Portfolio Management Techniques Course, 110
Portfolio manager, 50, 52, 65, 96, 102, 107
Portfolio theory, 110
Precedent transaction, 188
Principal repayment, 73
Principal, 52, 68, 72-74, 124, 138, 149, 168
Printing, 75, 177
Private companies, 13, 17, 30, 123, 136, 140, 141, 144, 148, 150, 152
Private equity, 7, 16-17, 20, 54, 75, 109, 111, 113, 123-126, 128, 130, 132, 134-136, 138-140, 142, 144, 146-152, 154, 156, 171, 188
Private placement, 45

Pro forma, 175-177, 188
Pro trading, 159
Profit, 13, 32, 34, 46, 59, 95, 105, 109, 117, 157-159, 163
Projection(s), 62, 139, 173-176, 180-182, 188
Prospectus, 18, 45, 188
Public company(ies), 13, 30, 33, 59, 75, 91, 123, 127, 136, 145, 171, 173, 176, 181-182, 188
Quarter(s), 13, 35, 173, 176, 187
Quarterly, 25, 62, 173, 176, 179
Quasi-equity, 17
Quasi-sale, 43
Quebec, 10, 12, 54, 72, 82, 86-87, 106, 121-122, 140, 147, 169-170
R&D, 126
Ratio, 45-46, 73, 75, 174, 187-188
RBC, 25, 50, 52, 57, 70, 72, 86, 88, 106, 121, 162, 168, 170
Real estate, 68, 77, 102, 109, 111, 138, 171
Receivables, 43, 75, 157, 178
Refinancing, 84
Registered representative(s), 91, 166
Rent, 187
Research analyst, 50, 52, 64
Restructuring, 42
Retail broker, 36, 48, 90-91, 93-94, 96-98, 102-105, 107
Retail broking, 6, 34, 48, 91, 93-95, 97, 99, 101, 103-105, 107, 109-110
Revenue, 13, 25, 32, 59, 62, 109, 174
Revolvers, 72
Risk, 27-28, 45, 48, 74, 76-77, 79-80, 82, 84, 96, 99, 103-104, 109, 111, 119, 127, 137, 144, 150-152, 154-155, 162-163, 165
Roadshow, 45

Rogers, 1718, 23
Rogers, Jimmy, 98
RRSP, 27
Salesman/men, 61-62, 80-81, 91, 94, 96
Sarbanes-Oxley Act, 32
Sceptic(s), 11
Sceptical, 77
Schedule I banks, 72, 86
Schedule II banks, 72, 86
Scotia, 54, 57, 68, 70, 72, 78, 82, 86, 88, 106, 121, 147, 150, 154, 156, 168, 170
Seasonal, 14, 75, 179
SEC, 35, 188
Secondary, 44, 132, 188
Securities law, 32, 45-46
Securitization, 43, 88-89
Sell side, 6, 41-42, 44, 46, 48, 50, 52, 54, 56, 58, 60, 62, 64, 66, 68, 70, 72, 74, 76, 78, 80, 82, 84, 86, 88, 90, 119
Senior debt, 14, 72, 75, 148, 150, 154, 190
Sensitivity tables, 182-184
Shareholder(s), 27-28, 30, 36, 42, 44, 116, 128, 137, 158, 178, 188
Short, 159
Software, 127, 130, 144
Spinning, 35
Spin-offs, 44
Spitzer, Eliot 34-35, 37
Steel, 177
Structured finance, 43
Subordinated debt, 74, 136
Sue, 45
Swaps, 157, 168
Syndication, 51, 75-76, 78, 93
Synergies, 36, 177
Target, 17, 21, 39, 45-46, 52, 62, 138, 148, 152, 154, 159
Tax, 26-29, 32, 43, 104, 128, 136-137, 139, 178
T-bills, 91

Index

TD, 57, 70, 72, 86, 88, 121, 147, 150, 156, 168, 170
Teachers, 18, 72, 87, 109, 121, 135, 147, 170
Tech, 31, 63, 126
Telecom, 77, 127, 177
Third world, 77
Tier 1 money manager, 107-108
Tier 2 money manager, 107-110
Tier 3 money manager, 108-110
Tombstones, 23
Trader(s), 12, 59, 63, 77, 95, 113, 157-160, 162-168
Trading, 7, 12, 25, 34-35, 59, 63, 65, 95, 103, 119, 157-171
Treasurer, 52, 78, 162
Treasury, 127, 188
Trust (confidence), 36, 65-66, 79
Trust (institution) 102
Trust (legal entity), 25-29
Trustee, 26, 28
Underwriter(s), 18, 23, 51
Underwriting, 18, 35-36, 42, 60, 63, 79, 88-89, 188
Unitholders, 26, 28, 34
US, 31-32, 157, 188
Using Microsoft Excel 97, 183
Valuation, 13, 45, 55, 61, 119, 138, 174, 182
Value, 10, 33, 42-45, 81, 83-85, 97, 103, 111, 115, 123, 125, 133-134, 141, 162, 167, 179-182, 186-187
Vancouver, 11, 57-58, 70-71, 86-87, 106, 122, 135, 147, 156, 168-170
VC, 18, 126, 128, 133-135, 188
Venture capital, 7, 16-18, 91, 123, 125-129, 131-136, 144, 147, 151, 155, 171, 188, 190
Venture capitalist(s), 50, 123, 126-128, 130-134, 188
WACC, 186
Warrants, 149, 151
Whistle-blowers, 32
Wood Gundy, 88, 106

Working capital, 117, 178
Workouts, 77
WorldCom, 32
Wrap account, 97
Yellow Pages, 18